Jason Oddy

Geoff Dyer's books include *But Beautiful*, *Yoga for People Who Can't Be Bothered to Do It*, *The Ongoing Moment* (winner of an Infinity Award from the International Center of Photography), and, most recently, a novel, *Jeff in Venice, Death in Varanasi*. His many prizes include a Somerset Maugham Award, the E. M. Forster Award, and a Lannan Literary Fellowship. He lives in London.

Also by Geoff Dyer

Jeff in Venice, Death in Varanasi

The Ongoing Moment

Yoga for People Who Can't Be Bothered to Do It

Anglo-English Attitudes

Paris Trance

The Missing of the Somme

The Search

But Beautiful

The Colour of Memory

Ways of Telling: The Work of John Berger

Additional Praise for *Out of Sheer Rage*

"We have an eager appetite for descriptions of certain species of failing in the successful. . . . *Out of Sheer Rage* is just the book, and a very funny one, too, for people who are possessed by this morbid craving."
—Katherine A. Powers, *The Boston Sunday Globe*

"Dyer's brand of imaginative criticism illuminates a direction where literary criticism might go. If only we could have more fresh, delightful, energetic books such as Dyer's."
—Jenifer Berman, *Bomb*

"An entertaining and highly original portrait of the inner life of a D. H. Lawrence addict." —Alain de Botton

"In some ways, *Out of Sheer Rage* is Geoff Dyer's *8 1/2*: a brilliant wank." —Charles Taylor, *The Boston Phoenix*

"*Out of Sheer Rage* is about something other than Lawrence or Not Lawrence. . . . Its real point is Dyer's roundabout, tricky, discursive, and often witty ramblings on what it means to make a work of art or even an artistic statement in a postmodern culture."
—Richard Eder, *Los Angeles Times*

"A splendid study on procrastination, denial, rationalization, and writer's block . . . Heartily recommended."
—Janice Braun, *Library Journal*

"If there was a prize for the year's funniest book, then Geoff Dyer's *Out of Sheer Rage* would win it hands down."
—Tim Hulse, *The Independent on Sunday* (UK)

"Such a sprawling, good-natured mess of a book that one has to consult the Library of Congress information to find out just what exactly the book is. Literary study? Yes. Travel book? Yes. Personal memoir? Oh, yeah. The trouble is, none of these categories allows you to believe how funny the book is, and moreover, what a brilliant character study [it] is of its own author, to say nothing of its subject." —Joey Sweeney, *Philadelphia Weekly*

"A cross of so many genres that it's a kind of literary mutt, a mutt you'll want to take home with you ... This book elevates *mal du siècle* to *mal du millennium*."
—Carolyn Nizzi Warmbold, *The Atlanta Journal-Constitution*

OUT OF SHEER RAGE

Wrestling with D. H. Lawrence

GEOFF DYER

Picador

Farrar, Straus and Giroux
New York

OUT OF SHEER RAGE. Copyright © 1997 by Geoff Dyer. All rights reserved. Printed in the United States of America. For information, address Picador, 175 Fifth Avenue, New York, N.Y. 10010.

www.picadorusa.com

Picador® is a U.S. registered trademark and is used by Farrar, Straus and Giroux under license from Pan Books Limited.

For information on Picador Reading Group Guides, please contact Picador. E-mail: readinggroupguides@picadorusa.com

Grateful acknowledgment is made to the following for their kind permission to reproduce copyrighted material: Laurence Pollinger Limited and the Estate of Frieda Lawrence Ravagli for quotations from the works and letters of D. H. Lawrence; Farrar, Straus and Giroux, Inc., for the excerpt from "Questions of Travel" in *The Complete Poems 1927–1979* by Elizabeth Bishop, copyright © 1979, 1983 by Alice Helen Methfessel; and Jeremy Reed for the quotation from "The Return."

ISBN 978-0-312-42946-1

Originally published by Little, Brown and Company, Great Britain

First published in the United States by Farrar, Straus and Giroux per – you see I *can* speak Italian – Valeria

'Out of sheer rage I've begun my book on Thomas Hardy. It will be about anything but Thomas Hardy I am afraid – queer stuff – but not bad.'

D. H. Lawrence, 5 September, 1914

'Endless explanations of irrelevancies, and none whatever of things indispensable to the subject.'

        Gustave Flaubert on Victor Hugo's Les Miserables

'It must all be considered as though spoken by a character in a novel.'

        Roland Barthes

Out of Sheer Rage

Looking back it seems, on the one hand, hard to believe that I could have wasted so much time, could have exhausted myself so utterly, wondering when I was going to begin my study of D. H. Lawrence; on the other, it seems equally hard to believe that I *ever* started it, for the prospect of embarking on this study of Lawrence accelerated and intensified the psychological disarray it was meant to delay and alleviate. Conceived as a distraction, it immediately took on the distracted character of that from which it was intended to be a distraction, namely myself. If, I said to myself, if I can apply myself to a sober – I can remember saying that word 'sober' to myself, over and over, until it acquired a hysterical, near-demented, ring – *if* I can apply myself to a sober, academic study of D. H. Lawrence then that will force me to pull myself together. I succeeded in applying myself but what I applied myself to – or so it seems to me now, now that I am lost in the middle of what is already a far cry from the sober academic study I had envisaged – was to pulling apart the thing, the book, that was intended to make me pull myself together.

I had decided years earlier that I would one day write a book about D. H. Lawrence, a homage to the writer who had made me want to become a writer. It was a cherished ambition and as part of my preparation for realising this cherished ambition I had avoided reading anything by Lawrence so that at some point in the future I could go back to him if not afresh then at least not rock-stale. I didn't want to go back to him passively, didn't want to pick up a copy of *Sons and Lovers* aimlessly, to pass the time. I wanted to read him with a purpose. Then, after years of avoiding Lawrence, I moved into the phase of what might be termed pre-preparation. I visited Eastwood, his birthplace, I read biographies, I amassed a hoard of photographs which I kept in a once-new document wallet, blue, on which I had written 'D.H.L.: Photos' in determined black ink. I even built up an impressive stack of notes with Lawrence vaguely in mind but these notes, it is obvious to me now, actually served not to prepare for and facilitate the writing of a book about Lawrence but to defer and postpone doing so. There is nothing unusual about this. All over the world people are taking notes as a way of postponing, putting off and standing in for. My case was more extreme for not only was taking notes about Lawrence a way of putting off writing a study of – and homage to – the writer who had made me want to become a writer, but this study I was putting off writing was itself a way of putting off and postponing another book.

Although I had made up my mind to write a book about Lawrence I had also made up my mind to write a novel, and while the decision to write the book about Lawrence was made later it had not entirely superseded that earlier decision. At first I'd had an overwhelming urge to write both books but these two desires had worn each other down to the point where I had no urge to write either. Writing them both at the same time was inconceivable and so these two equally overwhelming ambitions first wore each other down and then wiped each other out. As soon as I thought about working on the novel I fell to thinking that it would be much more enjoyable to write my study of Lawrence. As soon as I started making notes on Lawrence I realised I was probably sabotaging forever any chance of writing my novel which, more than any other book I had written, had to be written immediately, before another protracted bout of labour came between me and the idea for what I perceived as a rambling, sub-Bernhardian rant of a novel. It was now or never. So I went from making notes on Lawrence to making notes for my novel, by which I mean I went from not working on my book about Lawrence to not working on the novel because all of this to-ing and fro-ing and note-taking actually meant that I never did any work on either book. All I did was switch between two – empty – files on my computer, one conveniently called C:\DHL, the other C:\NOVEL, and sent myself ping-ponging back and forth between them until, after an hour and a half of this, I would turn off the computer because the worst thing of all, I knew, was to wear myself out in this way. The best thing was to do nothing, to sit calmly, but there was no calm, of course: instead, I felt totally desolate because I realised that I was going to write neither my study of D. H. Lawrence nor my novel.

Eventually, when I could bear it no longer, I threw myself wholeheartedly into my study of Lawrence because, whereas my novel was going to take me further into myself, the Lawrence book – a sober academic study of Lawrence –

would have the opposite effect, of taking me out of myself.

I felt happy because I had made up my mind. Now that I had made up my mind to throw myself wholeheartedly into one of the possible books I had been thinking about writing I saw that it didn't actually matter *which* book I wrote because books, if they need to be written, will always find their moment. The important thing was to avoid awful paralysing uncertainty and indecision. Anything was better than that. In practice, however, 'throwing myself wholeheartedly' into my study of Lawrence meant making notes, meant throwing myself *half*-heartedly into the Lawrence book. In any case, 'throwing myself wholeheartedly into my study of Lawrence' – another phrase which became drained of meaning as it spun round my head – was actually impossible because, in addition to deciding whether or not I was going to write my study of Lawrence, I had to decide where I was going to write it – *if* I was going to write it. *'If'* not *when* because once my initial euphoric resolve had collapsed the possibility of writing the novel made itself felt again as an attractive option. And even if I didn't decide to write my study of Lawrence I still had to decide where I was going to live because, irrespective of whether or not I was going to write my study of Lawrence, I still had to live somewhere – but if I *was* going to write a book about Lawrence then that brought in a whole range of variables which I would need to weigh up when considering where to live, even though deciding where to live was already complicated by a massive number of variables.

One of the reasons, in fact, that it was impossible to get started on either the Lawrence book or the novel was because I was so preoccupied with where to live. I could live anywhere, all I had to do was choose – but it was impossible to choose because I could live anywhere. There were no constraints on me and because of this it was impossible to choose. It's easy to make choices when you have things hampering you – a job, kids' schools – but when all you have to go on is your own desires, then life becomes considerably more difficult, not to say intolerable.

Even money wasn't an issue since at this stage I was living in Paris and nowhere could have been more expensive than Paris. The exchange rate got worse by the month and Paris became more expensive by the month. Money *was* an issue insofar as it made me think I would rather be anywhere than Paris but in terms of where to go next, where to move to, it was almost irrelevant. What the money situation – more exactly, the exchange rate situation – in Paris did was to emphasise that although I thought I had settled in Paris, really I had just been passing through, extremely slowly. That is all anyone English or American can do in Paris: pass through. You may spend ten years passing through but essentially you are still a sightseer, a tourist. You come and go, the waiters remain. The longer I stayed the more powerful it became, this feeling that I was just passing through. I had thought about subscribing to Canal Plus as a way of making myself feel more settled but what was the point in subscribing to Canal Plus when, in all probability, I would be moving on in a few months? Obviously the way to make myself more settled was to acquire some of the trappings of permanence but there never seemed any point acquiring the aptly named trappings of permanence when in a couple of months I might be moving on, might well be moving on, would almost certainly be moving on, because there was nothing to keep me where I was. Had I acquired some of the trappings of permanence I might have stayed put but I never acquired any of the trappings of permanence because I knew that the moment these trappings had been acquired I would be seized with a desire to leave, to move on, and I would then have to free myself from these trappings. And so, lacking any of the trappings of permanence, I was perpetually on the brink of potential departure. That was the only way I could remain anywhere: to be constantly on the brink not of actual but of potential departure. If I felt settled I would want to leave, but if I was on the brink of leaving then I could stay, indefinitely, even though staying would fill me with still further anxiety because, since I appeared to be staying, what was the point in living as though I were not staying but merely passing through?

These were all issues I intended to address, in different ways, either in mediated form in my study of Lawrence or, directly, in my novel, or vice versa, but there was an additional practical complication too. Since I was obliged to spend a certain amount of time away from wherever I lived, and since the rent on my Paris apartment was so high (and, because of the exchange rate, was becoming higher every month) I was frequently obliged to sub-let it (strictly speaking to sub-sub-let it since I was sub-letting it myself) and since, if you are sub-letting your apartment, you do not want to acquire too many valuable or personal items which might get destroyed, it then comes about that you yourself are living in conditions arranged primarily for those sub-letting from you: effectively, you are sub-letting from yourself. That's what I was doing: sub-letting from myself (strictly speaking, sub-sub-letting), living in an apartment devoid of anything that might have made it my apartment in the sense of my home. I had conspired to arrange for myself the worst of all possible worlds and my days were spent in this unbreakable circle of anxiety, always going over the same ground, again and again, always with some new variable, but never with any change. I had to do something to break this circle and so, when Marie Merisnil from whom I was sub-letting my apartment said that she wanted to give up the apartment because she was marrying the awful Jean-Louis whom I loathed even though he had once lent me a pair of elegant, pale blue pyjamas when I was in hospital for a few days, I decided to sign a contract that would make me the official tenant (as opposed to the illegal sub-tenant). I wasn't even sure that I wanted to stay in an apartment where I had actually been extremely unhappy for ninety per cent of my stay, where ninety per cent of my stay had been dominated by anxiety about (a) whether I *was* going to stay and (b) whether I was going to start a novel or start my study of Lawrence, but as soon as the managing agents said that they were unwilling to let the place to me – a foreigner with no job and no steady income, I was a poor prospect in anyone's eyes, even my own – I became convinced that I had to stay in this apartment where I had been sublimely happy, that there was, in fact, nowhere else on earth where I could hope to be as content. Eventually my rich friend, Hervé Landry ('Money Landry', as I liked to call him), owner of several houses, including one on the Greek island of Alonissos, agreed to stand as guarantor. The managing agents relented, and I signed the lease that made me the official *locataire*.

I was ecstatic. For about five minutes. Then I realised I had taken on an awesome, not to say crippling responsibility.

And far from solving the problem of where to live I had actually put a lid on it so that now my uncertainty was boiling away under pressure, threatening to blow me apart. The one thing I could be sure of was that I had to leave this apartment, where I had never known a moment's peace of mind, as soon as possible. If I stayed here, I saw now, I would fail to write both my novel and my study of Lawrence. That much was obvious. The trouble, the rub, was that I had to give three months' notice and therefore had to predict how I would be feeling three months hence which was very difficult. It was all very well deciding today that I wanted to leave but what counted was how I was going to be feeling three months from now. You could be perfectly happy today, I would say to myself, and three months from now you could be suicidal, precisely because you will see the enormity of the mistake you made by not renouncing the lease three months earlier. On the other hand, I would say to myself, you could be in utter despair today, convinced that another day in this apartment would kill you, convinced that it would be impossible to make any progress with your novel or your study of Lawrence and in three months' time you could see that it was only by remaining here that you survived the depression which will undoubtedly engulf you the moment you quit the apartment, as the rash act of renunciation committed three months previously will oblige you to do. Round and round I went, making no progress, resolving one thing one moment and another the next. 'I can't bear it any longer,' I would say to myself in the way that people always say 'I can't bear it any longer' to themselves, as a way, that is, of enabling them to go on bearing the unbearable. Eventually I really could bear it no longer, not for another second, and so I wrote to the agents and officially renounced the flat, claiming that 'professional' reasons had obliged me to return to England. The agents wrote back acknowledging my decision to leave the apartment. I wrote back saying that professional reasons now obliged me to remain in Paris. Could I therefore un-renounce my apartment? Relieved to be free of the trouble of re-letting it, the agents agreed to let me remain in the apartment which I had just renounced. And so it went on: I wrote again to renounce the apartment 'definitively'. They sent a somewhat curt acknowledgement of my decision. I wrote back changing my definitive decision to leave to a definitive decision to stay but it was too late, I had to leave.

Now that I *did* have to leave I was faced with the terrible prospect of having nowhere to live, of having to decide where to live without delay, and only then did I realise how much this apartment meant to me, how it *had* actually become my home. Although I'd believed that I had hardly any of my things in this apartment there were actually many of my own things that I now had to find a place for. Over the years I had actually acquired quite a few of the trappings of permanence. I even owned a surprising amount of furniture, some of it rather nice. Where was I going to store it? And what about me? Where was I going to store myself? Rome was a possibility. Laura, my almost-wife, had a lovely apartment in Rome and was always arguing in favour of our settling there but though Rome was an excellent place to spend time, I knew how depressed I always became there after a couple of months, especially during the winter. And even before I became depressed I knew how irritating I always found Rome, essentially because of the irrational closing times of shops, and the way films are dubbed into Italian. Still, Rome was a possibility – or would have been had Laura not sub-let *her* apartment. She had come to work in Paris for six months, partly to be with me, partly because this nice offer of work had come her way, but now she was back in Rome, subletting an apartment from someone else because her own apartment was sub-let. This is the true condition of western society on the brink of the millennium: everyone sub-letting from everyone else, no one quite sure whether they are leaving or staying, torn between being settlers and nomads, ending up as sub-letters. In the next few weeks she had to decide whether to continue to sub-let her flat or to move back in – and that depended in part on what I wanted to do because although we were used to spending a good deal of time apart we both felt that the moment had come when we should spend more time together, should even think about 'making our lives together' on a daily as well as an emotional basis. We already had our shared motto, almost shared, more accurately, because whereas Laura's version was 'Together Forever' mine was 'Together Whenever'. Laura liked the idea of us sticking together 'through thick and thin' whereas I opted for the more pessimistic 'through thin and thinner'. I was more than ready to put these semantic differences aside since if I was ever going to make any progress with my book about Lawrence – and get a reasonable shot at happiness into the bargain – I knew I would have to 'throw in my lot' with a woman as Lawrence had done with Frieda. Besides, I had already spent far too much time on my own. If I spent much more time on my own I would end up spending the rest of my life on my own. Even my crippling indecisiveness was primarily a symptom of having spent so much time on my own.

In a couple decisions are argued and debated; when you are alone there is no one to argue and debate with. To render my solitude bearable, therefore, I had internalised the dynamic of a couple who spent their time bickering ceaselessly about where to live and what to do. The problem was that the woman with whom I going to throw in my lot was also chronically indecisive and it was only my still greater indecisiveness that led her to believe that she was the kind of woman who knew her own mind and stuck to her guns. Although she often argued in favour of living in Rome, for example, she was always thinking about settling in Paris, her favourite city, and frequently pined for America where she had grown up.

I pined for it too. I thought of New York where I had lived and New Orleans where I had sort of lived, and San Francisco where I would love to live and where Laura had grown up, but even as I thought of these places I knew I would not go to live in any of them, especially New Orleans which I thought of and pined for on an almost daily basis. Even though I had such fond memories of sitting by the Mississippi I knew that I would never live in New Orleans again. Even though at some point in the day I always found myself wishing I was back in New Orleans, sitting by the Mississippi, I knew that I would never live there again and this knowledge made me feel that my life was over with. I am the kind of person, I thought to myself, who will spend the rest of his life saying 'I lived in New Orleans for a while' when in fact what I meant was that I had spent three months there, dying of loneliness, banging away at some useless novel simply for the companionship afforded by writing.

So where *were* we to live? More exactly – habits of solitude and selfishness die hard – where was the best place for *me* to live in order to make progress with my study of Lawrence? One of the reasons I had become so unsettled in Paris was because it had only a tangential connection with Lawrence. Paris was an excellent place to write a novel, especially a novel set in Paris, but it was not a good place to write a study of Lawrence. He hated Paris, called it, in fact, 'the city of dreadful night' or some such (I had the exact phrase in my notes somewhere). If I was to make any progress with my study of Lawrence, if I was to stand any chance of making any progress with my study of Lawrence, I knew that I had to live in a place which had some strong connection with him, a place where I could, so to speak, feel the Lawrentian vibes: Sicily, for example, or New Mexico, Mexico, Australia. The choice was immense because *Lawrence* couldn't make up his mind where to live. In the last years of his life he was always writing to friends asking if they had any ideas about where he might live. '*Where* does one want to live? Have you any bright ideas on the subject? Did you get a house west of Marseilles, as you said? How is it there?' On this occasion he was asking William Gerhardie. A little later it was an ex-neighbour from Florence: 'Where does one want to live? Tell me if you can! – how do you like London?' Then it was Ottoline Morrell's turn: 'Where does one want to live, finally?'

I had made this list of examples of Lawrence's anxiety about where to live because it reassured me in my own uncertainty; either it had reassured me or it had led me to become undecided, I was not sure. It was impossible to say. Who can tell? Perhaps the inability to decide where to live which I saw as one of the factors in preventing my making any progress with my study of Lawrence was actually part of my preparation for beginning to write it.

The one place I could be sure I couldn't write my study of Lawrence was England, which was a shame because I was actually feeling drawn to England. I was thinking of English telly in fact. I had an urge to be back there, watching telly, but moving back to England meant moving back into what, in my notes, I referred to by the Lawrentian phrase 'the soft centre of my being'. Being abroad – anywhere – meant being at the edge of myself, of what I was capable of. In England, for one thing, I could speak English whereas if I went to Rome I would be linguistically stranded. Not like Lawrence who had fluent Italian. He had a knack for languages (at one point he even began learning Russian from a grammar book) and although he claimed to hate speaking foreign languages, that was late in the day, by which time he had learnt several and had become weary of shifting from one to another. For my part I had not even attempted to learn French for the first six months of my time in Paris because it had seemed inconceivable that I could ever learn a foreign language. During that period my most intense relationships were all with cats and dogs, creatures with whom I could establish a bond of non-verbal sympathy. Since then I had picked up a bit of French, rather a lot actually, enough, certainly, to express grammatically wayward opinions. In fact now, after months of struggling to cope with the most rudimentary situations, now that I was on the brink of leaving, there was nothing I loved more than speaking French. By my standards I was fluent in French and speaking this garbled version of fluent French was one of the great sources of happiness in my life. Unless, that is, I was in a temper – which I was frequently. I could not express anger in French and this made me frustrated and angry and to express this anger and frustration I had to resort to English. In Rome I would be back to square one.

In Rome there was no chance of learning Italian because Laura is bilingual and has even more of a knack for languages than Lawrence. This is one of the things I first loved about Laura. Falling in love with Laura and all her languages was in some ways a premonition of the way that I would myself come to love speaking foreign languages, French specifically. Laura's method of learning a new language is to watch soap operas in that language. After a couple of episodes she has the simpler tenses off pat and within a week she is fluent. She is consequently a very poor teacher of Italian and I could see that after six months of watching soaps in Rome I would still speak barely a word of Italian because although I love the idea of speaking foreign languages I hate doing anything in life that requires an effort. Over the years I had got out of the habit of doing anything that required any effort whatsoever and so there was no chance of learning Italian and scarcely any prospect of getting on with my study of Lawrence which would require a massive, not to say Herculean labour.

I fretted and wondered. I sold my furniture and each day my apartment became less homely. Laura was pressing me for a decision because she had to make a decision about her apartment. Was I coming to Rome or not? More to the point, why was I even prevaricating like this? I was mad not to go to Rome, Rome was in Italy, the country where the Lawrences had spent more time than any other; it was within easy reach of Sicily where he had lived, and if I was to stand any chance of making any progress with my study of Lawrence it was probably the very best place I could be.

As soon as I arrived I knew I had made the right decision. My mind was made up: I was ready to begin my study of Lawrence. The only trouble was the heat. The heat was tremendous and nowhere in Rome was hotter than Laura's apartment. She had been so pleased to get back into her own place that she had forgotten how hot it would be. Heat is like that. In the course of winter unbearable heat cools in memory and becomes attractive, desirable. Now it was terribly hot. Even the light was hot. We tried to keep the light at bay, but it drilled through the keyhole, squeezed under the door, levered open the smallest of cracks in the shutters. My mind was made up, I was ready to work – but it was too hot to work. It was so hot we spent our waking hours dozing and our sleeping hours lying awake, trying to sleep. We were in a kind of trance. Then, one infernal night, Hervé called – a bad line – and invited us to spend the summer with him and Mimi on Alonissos, which was where he was calling from. 'What do you think?' Laura asked, but her eyes had already decided.

'I'll learn Greek,' she said. She had been eager to get back to her apartment but now she was desperate to leave. From my point of view six weeks on a Greek island, relatively speaking a *cool* Greek island, seemed a lovely prospect: the perfect time and the perfect place to begin my book on D. H. Lawrence. That's what I'll do, I said to myself, I'll start my study of D. H. Lawrence in Alonissos. It was the perfect place. I had everything I needed except my edition of *The Complete Poems* which I had left with a friend in Paris. Not that it mattered: just before the British Council Library in Rome had closed for the summer I had taken out several volumes of the Cambridge edition of Lawrence's letters and they would keep me going for a good while. I had a biography to check dates, copies of a few of the novels . . . It was perfect. According to Hervé, Laura and I would have a room to ourselves where, in the mornings, I could begin writing my study of D. H. Lawrence. It was perfect. It *would* have been helpful to have had my edition of *The Complete Poems* with me but it was not indispensable to my *beginning* the study. The important thing was that I had this chunk of uninterrupted time with no distractions. I should have taken out Volume 4 of the Cambridge edition of Lawrence's letters from the British Council Library, but Volumes 2 and 3, which I *did* get out, were certainly enough to be going on with. I was more concerned about not having my edition of *The Complete Poems* which, for my purposes, was probably the single most important book of Lawrence's, without which I would be able to make only very limited progress on my study of Lawrence, such limited progress, in fact, that it would be scarcely worth starting. My copy of *The Complete Poems* was crammed with notes and annotations and without it I was probably better off relaxing on Alonissos, gathering my strength and marshalling my ideas on Lawrence rather than actually trying to write anything. Suddenly that book of poems which, until two weeks previously, had been by my side constantly for two months and which I hadn't even opened in that time – hence the decision to leave it in a box at a friend's house in Paris – seemed indispensable to any progress.

Fortunately a friend of that friend was flying from Paris to Rome and he agreed to pick up my copy. We met at the San

Calisto, I bought him a coffee and he handed over the book. Simple as that. It was not just a good feeling, being reunited with my copy of *The Complete Poems* on the night before we were flying to Alonissos: it was an omen, a clear sign that I was *meant* to start my study of Lawrence that summer.

After retrieving *The Complete Poems*, Laura and I headed home to pack. With all the books by and about Lawrence my luggage was incredibly heavy. Not just inconveniently so but excess baggagely so. I took out a few books that I didn't need, which I had only packed because they were thin – *Mornings in Mexico*, *Apocalypse* – but these were so light as to make no difference and I put them back in the bag I had just taken them out of. I looked at the copy of *The Complete Poems* and felt suddenly sure that if I took it to Alonissos it would lie unopened for six weeks just as it had lain unopened in Paris for two months; but if I didn't take it to Alonissos I was equally sure that, once I was there, in Alonissos, I would decide that it was indispensable and that, without it, I would be unable even to start my book on Lawrence. If I take it I won't need it; if I don't take it I will not be able to get by without it, I said to myself as I packed and unpacked my bag, putting in my copy of *The Complete Poems* and taking it out again. After a while I decided to leave *The Complete Poems* and pack the Penguin edition of the *Selected Poems* but that was a ludicrous compromise since the defining characteristic of the *Selected Poems* was that it contained none of the poems I needed, the 'Last Poems', principally, 'The Ship of Death' in particular. It was a straight choice – either the immense bulk of *The Complete Poems* or nothing – and, once I recognised that the real issue had nothing to do with whether or not I would need to refer to *The Complete Poems*, a very simple one. The value of *The Complete Poems* was talismanic: if I had it with me I would be able to begin my book; if I didn't have it with me then, even if I did not need to refer to it, I would keep thinking that I did and would be unable to begin my book about Lawrence. Put like that *The Complete Poems* was an essential part of my luggage. I had no choice but to bring it with me; whether I referred to it or not was entirely irrelevant. With that I put *The Complete Poems* on the top of the pile of essential books by and about Lawrence, pulled my rucksack's cord sphincter as tight as possible, and propped it by the door, ready for our departure first thing in the morning.

In the morning, before setting off, I took out my copy of *The Complete Poems* and left for Greece without it.

Another good decision, as it turned out. I didn't need *The Complete Poems* because once we were installed on Alonissos I had no impulse to begin my study of D. H. Lawrence anyway. It was not the availability or non-availability of books that was the problem, it was Alonissos itself. We always have this ideal image of being on an island but actually being on an island always turns out to be hellish. For what it is worth, Lawrence wasn't too keen on islands either. 'I don't care for islands, especially very small ones,' he decided on Île de Port Cros. A week later, as if, first time around, he had simply been trying out an opinion, and had now made up his mind, he announced, definitively: 'I *don't* like little islands.'

Me neither. All you can think of when you are on a small island is the impossibility of leaving when you want to, either because the island you are on is too big and you want to go to a smaller one or because the island is too small and you want to go to a bigger one. When we arrived at Alonissos on the Flying Dolphin the island seemed so beautiful that six weeks did not seem long enough to enjoy it to the full. Hervé's house had a lovely large terrace with a perfect view of sea and sky, the kind of view you see in posters advertising holidays on idyllic Greek islands.

'This is paradise,' I said to Laura, sitting on the terrace, surrounded by sea and sky. 'I wish we were going to be here for six months.' Then, after a week, even a fortnight seemed intolerable. Except for looking at the brochure-blue sea and sky – which, after the first couple of days, we scarcely even noticed – there was nothing to do and for that reason it was impossible to get any work done. The best circumstances for writing, I realised within days of arriving on Alonissos, were those in which the world was constantly knocking at your door; in such circumstances the work you were engaged in generated a kind of pressure, a force to keep the world at bay. Whereas here, on Alonissos, there was nothing to keep at bay, 'there was no incentive to generate any pressure within the work, and so the surrounding emptiness invaded and dissipated, overwhelmed you with inertia. All you could do was look at the sea and sky and after a couple of days you could scarcely be bothered to do that.

There was no use blaming my inability to get started on having left my copy of *The Complete Poems* in Rome because I had it beside me in Alonissos. Yes. At the last possible moment, with the taxi rumbling downstairs, I had dashed back up, retrieved my copy and lugged it all the way to Alonissos where, exactly as predicted, it lay unopened by our bed. Instead I found myself reading one of the books Hervé had brought along, a volume of Rilke's letters.

'*Il faut travailler, rien que travailler.*' Rilke had gone to Paris in 1902 to write a monograph on Rodin and this exhortation of the sculptor's had a transforming effect on the twenty-seven-year-old poet. In letter after letter he repeated Rodin's mantra-like injunction. Immerse yourself in your work: let life fall away, dedicate yourself to the great work. *Il faut travailler, rien que travailler.*

I found myself repeating it the way Rilke did, trying it out, enjoying the simplicity and faithfulness of the formula, luxuriating in it like a hot bath. Dwelling on it like this, however, was an evasion of work, just as my reading of a hefty volume of Rilke's letters was an indulgence. I should have been working on my study of D. H. Lawrence and instead I was idling over Rodin's words. *Il faut travailler, rien que travailler.* I should be writing my book about D. H. Lawrence, I said to myself, everything else should be subordinate to that – but who can tell where that task begins and ends? Some huge benefit may yet accrue from reading Rilke's letters. The more I read, in fact, the more convinced I became that a better understanding of Rilke was crucial to my understanding of Lawrence. Had I gone to Alonissos to write a book about Rilke then I would, almost certainly, have been sitting on Hervé's terrace reading books by Lawrence; as it was, the fact that I was meant to be starting my study of D. H. Lawrence meant that I was sitting there reading the letters of Rilke who, though he was seduced by and persuaded of the truth of Rodin's exhortation to do nothing but work, found it difficult to submit to it in practice: 'Already I am wavering in my absolute determination to shut myself up daily, wherever I am and in whatever external circumstances, for so-and-so-many hours for my work's sake.'

He also wavered about whether work and idleness could be so easily counterposed:

> I have often asked myself whether those days on which we are forced to be indolent are not just the ones we pass in profoundest activity? Whether all our doing, when it comes later, is not only the last reverberation of a great movement which takes place in us on those days of inaction...

Now that idea immediately took my fancy, that was an idea I liked a lot. So much so that after a few more days the Rilke letters went the way of *The Complete Poems* and lay unopened on our bedside table. Everything lay unopened in Alonissos, even the cover of my tennis racket. It was impossible to write on Alonissos, it was impossible to read, and it was impossible to play tennis. Laura found it impossible to make any progress with Greek. It was actually impossible to do anything. I had thought that after working on my book about Lawrence in the mornings I would spend the afternoons playing tennis but there were no courts and so, having spent the mornings not writing my book about Lawrence and not reading Rilke, I spent the afternoons not playing tennis. The last time I had been on a Greek island there were regular, ill-tempered matches between the tourists and the locals. Here there was no football and no tennis. In fact there was no anything. All you could do was eat lunch and jump into the jellyfish-infested sea from the snake-infested rocks of the *plaka*. We saw a snake there on our third day. Laura and I were walking through the little wood before you get to the rocks and we saw it at the same time. All my life I have dreaded seeing a snake and on Alonissos I saw one. We both saw it at the same time, turned on our heels and fled. Lawrence in his white pyjamas had a *rendezvous* with his snake; we fled from ours. I wasn't even sure what happened: either we saw it lying motionless and then, as a result of our panic, it suddenly sidled away or it heard us and began darting away and as a result of this movement we saw *it*. It all happened too fast: it saw us and fled, we saw it and fled; we hoped we never saw *it* again and *it* probably felt the same about us. Not exactly sentiments to make a poem out of.

After that we were nervous about being on the rocks of the *plaka* because although we saw the snake in the woods it was actually on the sun-warmed rocks of the *plaka* that the snakes, like us – like us before we saw the snake – liked to bask, like sharks. We were nervous about the sea anyway, because of the jellyfish, and now we were nervous about the rocks, because of the snakes. We were also nervous in bed. We lay there and heard slithery, rustling noises suggesting that things were slithering and rustling outside our door. We lay awake talking about what things they might be.

'I hate slithery things,' I said.

'I hate rustling things,' said Laura.

'Some things rustle *and* slither,' I said. It was an idiotic conversation and on one level I couldn't believe we were actually having it. On another level . . . on another level I still couldn't believe we were having it but eventually it wearied us to the point where we could sleep.

In the morning we had breakfast with Hervé and Mimi, an event dominated by *buzzing* things: wasps, swarms of them. They came for the honey and the jam. Mimi had a live-and-let-live policy. I wanted to slaughter them all – at least it would have been something to do – but Mimi argued that the best policy was to ignore them.

'Try ignoring them when you've been stung in the mouth, your tongue's swelling up, you're choking and you're looking round for someone who knows how to do an emergency tracheotomy,' I said. Seeing a wasp crawling over my plate I flattened it with a copy of the local, yoghurt-spotted Greek paper. Mimi looked at me. She was wearing a yellow and black head scarf which may be why I had half a mind to take a swipe at her too.

'Life is more vivid in the dandelion than in the green fern,' I said. 'Life is more vivid in the wasp than in the dandelion. Life is more vivid in me than the wasp. The wasp can devour the dandelion. I can destroy the wasp.' With that Laura and I got up to leave. We were so bored on Alonissos that tempers were getting somewhat frayed. There was nothing to do except pick quarrels with each other and drive faster and faster on the moped along the winding roads of the island. Now that *was* fun! Even though it was only fun because of the condition of almost catatonic boredom in which we found ourselves – and was itself, therefore, contaminated by boredom to some degree – it was still fun to drive round the island at speed. One way of keeping boredom at bay would have been to make a start on my book about Lawrence in much the same way that he had translated Giovanni Verga on the way to Ceylon and Australia, but making a start on Lawrence seemed more boring than doing nothing. Even writing a postcard required more concentration than I could muster. In a matter of days chronic boredom had come to seem the natural condition of existence and the only response to it was the bored one of zooming round the island on a moped.

In Rome Laura travelled by moped the whole time, it was her way of getting around the city, but in Alonissos we drove around just for the hell of it because there was nothing else to do. We sped along the deserted roads, throttle back, sky in our hair. In Rome I had been a nervous passenger and we had quarrelled many times because I was always shouting out warnings, alerting Laura to danger and thereby, she claimed, taking the fun out of one of the activities she most loved in life which was riding through Rome on her moped. Since there was no danger on Alonissos I even did some of the driving, something I never did in Rome. We leaned into curves, swept through bends, glided down the long inclines of hills, engine off. This proved a terrible mistake. The gradient was such that as we glided down one twisting hill, the moped accelerated with every bend until, just as Laura shouted, 'Careful!' we smashed into the cliff wall at 20 mph. Crumph! It was unbelievable. I sat on the floor, stunned. Laura was groaning. I just sat there, moaning and groaning, stunned, hearing Laura groaning.

'Did you hit your head?' I said.

'Yes,' moaned Laura. I just sat there, moaning and groaning. Whatever we didn't want to happen had already happened. It was already too late to do anything about it. One moment we were about to crash, the next moment we had crashed. The crash was wedged between these two moments. There wasn't even time for things to go into slow motion as they allegedly do in the build-up to a crash. Laura was lying on the floor, moaning, now she was sitting up and walking. I was sitting, moaning. A taxi stopped.

'We can take a taxi,' Laura said, as though we were late for a concert with no bus in sight. I got up. 'I can't move,' I said, moving towards the taxi. Everything was terrible and in the back of the taxi I kept saying sorry to Laura. Through the shock there were different kinds of hurt: the stinging of grazes which was nothing, the pain of cuts which was also almost nothing, the hurt of my hip which was less but worse, an ache in my back and, deeper within, hardly even perceptible as pain yet, there was a very dull ache of something that might be badly wrong. Laura was crying. I kept asking if she had hit her head and she said yes but there was no bump or blood or anything and so I said you can't have hit your head and she agreed. We got out, the taxi stopped and left. It was terrible, walking into the hospital which was not even a hospital, just a kind of dressing station where there were no doctors to be seen. Then one appeared, a doctor, or at least someone in a white coat, moving unhurriedly. Laura said her ribs hurt and I said, 'I am so sorry.' I sat there, on a chair, hurting everywhere, but differently in different places. The doctor-orderly took Laura into a room and she lay down while I sat there, not in the room with her but in the waiting room. I held myself together very carefully, not moving anything. I walked into the room where Laura was lying down because the doctor said her blood pressure was way up or way down because she was in shock, and after waiting a while it came down or went up to normal. Now I sat in the room with the couch or the bed where Laura was lying down and the doctor was cleaning out the cuts on her fingers. The stuff he was putting on her fingers hurt and she kicked her heels up and down on the bed. 'My ribs hurt,' she said, 'I think I've hurt my ribs.'

'Don't worry,' I said.

Then it was my turn. The doctor did things to my arms, cleaned out some cuts. He began putting stitches in my arm and Laura left the room. I have had so many stitches in my time that they did not worry me at all. Cuts don't really matter even though they hurt. It was the bits that were broken up inside, like my spleen which might have been ruptured, that worried me. My arm was stitched. I stood up. 'My hip hurts,' I said. The doctor took off my trousers and saw my hip was all gouged up and said, 'We'd better do something about that too.'

After all these repairs we sat and waited awhile. They had no X-rays at this little hospital and so there was nothing to be done about Laura's ribs which were hurting more and more, or my back which was beginning to hurt strangely. We sat and then we walked back home. A taxi took us back to the moped which I had thought we would ride back home but which turned out to be mangled and unrideable. We walked home and climbed in over the wall to our house. We got into bed, hurting everywhere.

From there on it got worse. As the day wore on the hurt set in. We hurt everywhere and we could not stop replaying the crash even though the thought of it made us both sick. The other thing we could not stop doing was having sex. We were in a terrible state but, for some reason, we were desperate to have sex. It was the shock I suppose. Neither of us could move properly but if we arranged ourselves, carefully, we could make each other come. I lay on my back and Laura moved over my face, saying 'Ah, my ribs!' when she came. We took it in turns to come and we took it in turns to say, 'How was it possible that we didn't hit our heads?' We kept saying this because the more we replayed the crash the more it seemed a miracle that we hadn't killed or paralysed ourselves. I kept saying, too, that I would never get on a moped again, ever, anywhere.

It was my fault, the crash, but Laura never reproached me about it. Had Laura been driving I would have held it against her, I would have nagged her about her reckless driving, how she had been on the brink of getting us killed in Rome and now, in Alonissos, had actually succeeded. As it was, the crash was my fault but at least I had taken the brunt of the impact. I had softened the blow for Laura and the reason my back hurt so much was probably because her head had banged into my spine. The last thing I wanted to think about was the moment of impact but that word 'impact' and the phrase 'the moment of impact' kept repeating themselves in my head. That's all I could think of: the impact, the moment, the moment of impact.

The next morning I could not move. I had to be helped out of bed. I couldn't move. My back, I said, my back and my neck. My hip was murder, my hands and arms smarted, but it was my back that worried me. We went to see the osteopath, an Australian woman whose hands inched up and down my spine, her fingers performing a manual X-ray, feeling her way through the skin to the bones beneath.

'It can't be anything too bad,' she said. 'If it was, you'd be in agony.'

'I am in agony,' I said, but not the kind of agony she had in mind. It was possible I had *cracked* a vertebra but that was all and even if I had cracked a vertebra there was nothing to be done about it anyway. It was the same with Laura and her ribs: even if her ribs *were* cracked all she could do was wait for them to get better. Reassured, we shuffled back home, Laura holding her ribs and me with my chin resting in my right hand, supporting it. To everyone else on the island it looked like I was deep in thought, wrestling with philosophical problems, when all I was doing was trying to bear the awful weight of my head – which, on reflection, is what all philosophical thought comes down to anyway: how to bear the awful weight of your head.

We were keen to leave Alonissos, and Hervé and Mimi were keen to get rid of us. One way and another we had pretty well ruined their stay on the island. Before leaving I tried to negotiate the return of at least part of my deposit from the guy who had rented us the moped. He wouldn't budge, not by a drachma. He took out great wads of drachmas from his till – mechanic's money: oil-smeared, disintegrating, held together by grease – and explained how impossible it was to make a living renting mopeds. At one point Lawrence says that 'the Italians are really rather low-bred swine nowadays'. He should have gone to Greece, should have hired and crashed a moped on Alonissos before making such an insulting generalisation – insulting to the Greeks, I mean, for they pride themselves on being swine.

Hervé and Mimi took us down to the Flying Dolphin. We had a difficult journey in front of us – boat, bus, plane, another plane, train, taxi – but not an impossible one. Luggage was a problem and so I left my copy of *The Complete Poems* behind, together with many other books by or about Lawrence. I had taken *The Complete Poems* to Alonissos and now that we were heading back to Rome where I would be housebound for God knew how long I would once again be without it. I didn't care. There was a curse on that book. I was better off without it.

*

Back in Rome people were using the word 'heatwave' even though it was the middle of August. I had two projects: one was to keep cool, the other not to sneeze. When I sneezed I felt like my spine was about to burst apart. Sneezing was terrifying and now that I could not do it any more I realised that I had always liked sneezing. Sneezing was one of life's little pleasures, one that I could no longer risk – like sleeping on my side. I had to sleep on my back, I had to try to sleep on my back and, as I lay awake on my back, trying to sleep, I kept thinking what a great pleasure it was to sleep on your side, to sleep first on one side and then, while you were still asleep, to roll over on to the other side. Laura had to lie on her back too and so we lay there, on our backs, thinking about the crash which we no longer thought of as an accident but as a miraculous escape. How could it have happened, how could we have got away with it? How could we have smacked straight into a cliff wall at at least 25 mph and not banged our heads, not broken anything? We were wearing only T-shirts and shorts and yet we broke nothing: we were bruised deeply but our spleens had not ruptured and our bones were not broken. We were not paralysed, we were not cabbages, we were not dead – we just had to lie on our backs and I had to avoid sneezing. It didn't even matter that we were confined to the apartment. All I had to do to get a feel of the neighbourhood, the *quartiere*, was hold my hand under the cold tap. First the water was warmish, room temperature, then cooler, then warm, as the pipes climbed down the walls into the apartment, hot as they moved over the sun-baked roof, warm again as they descended on the other side, in shadow, becoming cooler, and then cold, lovely black-cold, as they disappeared below ground, into the past.

Slowly we began to recover. In the evenings we limped to L'Obitorio for a pizza and then to our local bar, the San Calisto, where Fabrizio, the barman, had elevated surliness to the level of a comprehensive world view. With an unrelenting scowl, he abused everything he touched, yanking the lids off the *gelato*, gouging out the *gelato*, dumping it in glasses, thumping the glasses on the counter. To perform such simple actions with such aggression was no mean achievement but the truly remarkable thing was that he managed also to imbue them with a rough tenderness. His unfailing curtness — ah, how lovely it was to be on the receiving end of it! — was, likewise, a gesture of welcome. We liked to sit outside and listen to him preparing a cappuccino, hurling the saucer on to the zinc bar, tossing the spoon on to the saucer, chucking milk into the coffee, hurling the cup on to the saucer, and then throwing a hasty '*prego*' through the clatter and noise of his colleagues. He did this even when the Calisto was empty: it was a way of generating business, like the bell of an ice-cream van: a call to customers: 'The cappuccini are good here, we are always busy.'

We even got back on the moped. I had vowed never to get on a moped again but Laura, even in the dark days following the crash, conceded only that, back in Rome, she would be more careful, more alert. Now we were back in Rome she was eager, as she put it, 'to get back in the saddle'. Laura has a good attitude to life and that, even more than her ability to pick up languages by watching soap operas, is why I love her. I, by contrast, have a very bad attitude to life, an attitude to life that began badly and is getting worse with every passing year, but it was not difficult for Laura to persuade me to get on the moped again. Laura drove, carefully, trying to avoid jolts. In Piazza Venezia we paused to admire *il vigile*, the white-gloved policeman who directed traffic with movements of hypnotic elegance. From his podium he conducted the traffic like a symphony: beckoning, halting, directing. It was impossible to say where one gesture ended and the next began. 'Halt' – clearly stated, unequivocal – merged exquisitely into 'go' in one flowing movement. Each gesture was executed with a flourish but this flourish – this elaboration and amplification of what was strictly necessary – added to its clarity, to its geometric precision. So it was with the architectural flourishes of Rome's great baroque churches. The *vigile*'s gestures were so clear that he seemed to address cars individually, making drivers almost proud to obey his commands. The traffic responded so promptly it was easy to think he took his cue from their movements, so that his conducting became a form of dance.

From there we walked up the steps to the Campidoglio, Laura's favourite piazza.

'So what do you notice about this piazza?' she asked.

'It's full of tourists.'

'Anything else?'

'They're all wearing check trousers.'

'The *piazza*.'

'It's a perfect square.'

'And do you know why it's a perfect square?'

'No. Why?'

'Because it's not,' said Laura, explaining how Michelangelo had allowed for the foreshortening of perspective by elongating the far side of the square and compressing another part. Before I had time to wonder if a more general truth could be extrapolated from the example of the

Campidoglio we were off again, heading to Lungotevere to assume our place among the twenty or thirty mopeds waiting on lights, revving. At first, because of our Attic trauma, we kept to the uncrowded back of the grid and because our moped, a Piaggio Ciao, had very little acceleration we were among the last to crawl away from the lights. As the days went by and Laura became more confident she inched ahead until we were at the front of the grid. I was feeling more confident too.

'Get ready to go on the G of green,' I said.

'No,' said Laura, revving and roaring. 'On the D of red.'

After an initial period of silent contrition I was also feeling more confident about criticising Laura's driving. I once again started yelling out excited, nervous warnings: 'There's a bus ahead! Careful, there's a taxi coming in from the side! Pot-hole! Watch out, car behind!'

'Of course there's a car behind, of course there's a bus ahead,' said Laura, unperturbed by the metal converging on us from all sides. 'This is a city, what do you expect?'

The problem with Alonissos, Laura assured me, was that it was not a city, the roads were deserted and this is why it had been so dangerous – whereas riding a moped in Rome was so obviously filled with peril and danger that it was actually quite safe. Which was why, she went on, it was perfectly okay to get stoned and *then* go for a ride and see the city veer by in a series of near-misses.

It was still blazing hot. The only way to cool down was to stop for a *grattachecca* near Isola Tiberina. Glasses were crammed with ice-scrapings, and fruit juice poured over the ice. There was always a queue, even at three in the morning. One boy's job was to scrape away at a vast block of ice. Laura noticed that he had an unappetising plaster on one frozen finger. It was hard to imagine how cold his hands must have been, colder than a fishmonger's even, but that was how he scraped a living.

There was one other cool place, a building on Via Manunzio that we were drawn to, reluctantly, repeatedly. Everywhere around was boiling hot but this one building gave off an icy chill. On the door someone had written, in English, 'Undertakers'. We went there often and then accelerated away, spooked, heading somewhere else, happy to be on the moped again.

Everything made us happy. We were getting better. We were full of 'the intoxication of convalescence', full, as Nietzsche said, of 'reawakened faith in tomorrow and the day after tomorrow, of a sudden sense and anticipation of a future, of impending adventures, of seas that were open again, of goals that were permitted again, believed again'.

I believed again in my study of Lawrence, even suspected that it had been my destiny to go to Alonissos, read (a little) Rilke, crash the moped and discover this affinity with Lawrence. According to Huxley, who knew him well, Lawrence's great responsiveness to the world came from the way his 'existence was one long convalescence, it was as though he were newly reborn from a mortal illness every day of his life'. In one of the letters I had read on Alonissos, Rilke too, had written of 'the long convalescence which is my life'. The four of us – Nietzsche, Rilke, Lawrence and I – were bound together by a shared convalescence. Before the crash in Alonissos I had made no progress on my study of Lawrence; now, in the euphoria of convalescence, I was raring to go. The problem was that, apart from the volumes of letters from the British Council Library, I had no books by Lawrence: I had left them all in Alonissos. Hervé had said he would post them on to us but who could say how long that would take? The post between Italy and England was terrible (Lawrence gnashed his teeth about it the whole time) so God alone knew what the post between Alonissos and Italy was like. For all I knew my books could take months to arrive.

This was a real stroke of luck. Because I was unable to consult the books I needed, because, without them, I was in no position to make any progress with my study, I took to leafing through my collection of photos of Lawrence. That's when I realised I was more interested in photos of Lawrence than in the books he wrote.

'Michelet wrote nothing about anyone without consulting as many portraits and engravings as he could.' Imitating his subject's habit, Roland Barthes obtained all available portraits of Michelet in the course of writing his book about him. Thinking specifically of Auden, Joseph Brodsky said that after reading a certain amount of work by a given writer we become curious to know what he or she looks like. In the case of Lawrence my curiosity had been satisfied before it was even awakened; likewise the Michelet–Barthes practice of accumulating pictures of one's subject: this task had been carried out unsystematically, randomly, before I got down to the serious business of putting off writing my study of him. It was in Rome, while I was convalescing, leafing through photographs, that I realised that I actually had a *collection* of photographs of Lawrence. Over the years collecting photos of Lawrence had been one of my many little hobbies, the sum total of which gave me a sense of purpose that counteracted my usual purposelessness. In second-hand shops I was always sniffing around in the Lawrence section, primarily for a copy of the Penguin edition of *Phoenix* (long out of print) that I had been hunting down for many years, but also for any books with pictures of Lawrence. Whenever I came across a new book about Lawrence, even the kind of dismal academic criticism I would never have dreamed of reading, I flicked through it in case there were some photos I had not seen before, or, ideally, a photo which I *had* seen before, when I was seventeen, and which I had not seen since.

What I might do, it occurred to me in Rome, was prepare an album of these pictures, arrange them in a fashion that pleased me – interspersing them, when appropriate, with pictures of my family and myself – provide captions (lengthy ones, quite often) and then, late in the day, remove the pictures so that only the captions and the ghosts of photos remained. And not to stop there: to rearrange these captions so that they referred only occasionally to the photographs for which they had been intended, so that they existed, instead, in relation to each other – *that*, I thought to myself, might not only enable me to get started on my study but even prevent my falling into idleness and depression for a while.

The more I looked at my collection of Lawrence photographs, the more insistent became the feeling that *I did not know what Lawrence looked like*. The photographs posed exactly the question they proposed to answer: what did D. H. Lawrence look like? By all accounts his beard was red; in photographs it was black. Lawrence himself grumbled about this. 'I hate photographs and things of myself, which are never me, and I wonder all the time who it can be. Look at this passport photograph I had taken two days ago, some sweet fellow with a black beard I haven't got.' Uncertainty regarding the appearance of Lawrence the man *as he actually was* is counterbalanced by an enduring, iconic image of Lawrence the writer. Hence that strange sense that the painted portraits of the true-to-life, red-bearded man – like the one by Jan Juta on the cover of the Penguin *Selected Poems* – did not look like D. H. Lawrence.

I'd bought that edition of poems – the one I had not taken to Alonissos and which, consequently, I had with me in Rome – in Blackwells when we were 'doing' Lawrence at college. I may have looked very different then but even in 1977, close on twenty years ago, it seems to me, *I looked like myself*. We all believe this: at every moment in our lives, we look like ourselves; others, whom we have not met, whom we know only through photographs, become fixed at certain intervals. We know them only as they appear in these photographs. As authors continue to publish books the jacket photos are usually updated every few years: a given photograph corresponds to a given book, or a certain phase of work. In the case of dead authors one or two pictures come to stand for the entire life: all of Scott Fitzgerald's books were written by the fresh-faced, unsozzled Scottie; all of Henry James's by the bald magister. The longer the life, the greater the output, the more intense the degree of photographic compression: a single photograph of Dickens is sufficient to accommodate thirty years and tens of thousands of pages of work. Such a photograph serves to consolidate – to embody – the idea of the writer whose death was announced in a famous essay of Barthes. Or, to put it in terms consistent with this notion, a photograph of a writer is not really a photograph of a person but an emblem – a colophon – of the works published under his or her name. Inevitably a considerable degree of distortion takes place when a single photograph represents a working life covering several decades.

David Herbert Lawrence began to look like D. H. Lawrence the writer when he grew his beard in the autumn of 1914. 'I've been seedy, and I've grown a red beard,' he wrote, 'behind which I shall take as much cover henceforth as I can, like a creature under a bush.' Lawrence may have wanted to hide behind his beard but in doing so he became permanently identified by it, revealed himself in hiding ('I send a passport photograph of myself, but you'd know us anyhow – my beard').

Lawrence without his beard was not D. H. Lawrence. In a picture taken for his twentieth birthday – 'clean-shaven, bright young prig in a high collar like a curate', as Lawrence himself put it, less than two months before his death, 'guaranteed to counteract all the dark and sinister effect of all the newspaper photographs' – he didn't look like D. H. Lawrence: he looked like the man who would go on to become D. H. Lawrence. He looked properly like D. H. Lawrence only when, in the words of Marguerite Yourcenar's Hadrian, it was possible to discern in him the profile of his approaching death. The closer he came to dying the more he looked like D. H. Lawrence. A photograph taken at the Chalet Kesselmatte in 1928 showed him with his sister Emily. Her robustness emphasised his own emaciated, desiccated condition. His clothes hung on him, he was shrinking into them. There was almost no flesh to soften the contact between the bones of his legs and the wooden slats of the bench; the only padding was provided by the trousers which lay in folds around his thighs. The fabric, it seemed, was thicker than the man beneath it. He clutched the wrist of his right arm with his left hand, holding himself together. The face was drying out, like clay. A few months later, in February, writing to Emily from Vence, he harked back to the time of that photograph as if to a period of robust well-being: 'I had to give in and come – Dr Morland insisted so hard, and I was losing weight so badly, week by week. I only weigh something over six stones – and even in the spring I was over seven, nearly eight.'

In death Lawrence became identical with his canonic image. Death fixed the image, rendered it – and the body of work of which it was the symbolic expression – incapable of further development. That is why Lawrence, like Rilke, hated photographs of himself. To both writers photographs prefigured an end of becoming.

Virtually the final creative act Lawrence was involved in before his death at the sanatorium at Vence was to sit for a bust by the sculptor Jo Davidson. The last photo I had of Lawrence was not of the man but of the living-death mask that resulted from these sessions. 'Jo Davidson came and made a clay head of me – made me tired,' Lawrence moaned in a postscript to his very last letter, 'result in clay mediocre.' It was anything but that, but it is not surprising that Lawrence responded like this, was reluctant, even at this late stage, to recognise the stark fact of his own mortality: what must it have been like to see his death take shape, to become fully formed, undeniable like this? To have seen a death mask of himself while still – just – alive? 'What do I care for first or last editions?' he had asked, rhetorically, years earlier. 'To me, no book has a date, no book has a binding.' No wonder he was hostile to Davidson's bust: it anticipated – if only by a few days – the form the loose pages of his life would take when bound and dated.

Among all these photos of Lawrence there was none of him at Fontana Vecchia, the house in Taormina, where he lived, off and on, from 1920–23. We were feeling so much better – Laura's ribs had healed completely, my back hurt only occasionally – and I was so fired up about my study of Lawrence that we decided to go there and take one.

For someone who has spent so much of her life on the move, Laura is strangely un-blasé about travelling. She packs days in advance, sets off with excess bags of time to spare and arrives at airports way before the check-in desks have opened; on the plane she scrutinises the in-flight safety video like a first-time flyer. On this occasion she was anxious that we had enough to eat on the train, enough *crackers* to eat on the train. She likes to eat crackers. She is crazy about crackers. Crackers and toffees. I persuaded her to make room for bread and *pomodori* and then we bickered about her camera. It's a Nikon, non-automatic, and weighs like something from another, weightier era of technology, which it is. Despite its weight Laura insists on taking it wherever we go – which is fine except that I then have to carry whatever extra weight has built up as a result of the camera. I don't carry the camera but I end up carrying its equivalent. Still, better that than the camera itself. The camera is the worst thing to carry. It's heavy and it keeps digging into you; it has about ten sharp angles and they all dig in. It's awkward as a spade, that camera. I hate it. I would like a lightweight modern automatic camera, the kind you can slip into a shirt pocket, the sort that doesn't dig in, but it is too late get one now. In the last five years I have been to all kinds of eminently photographable places but I've never had a camera with me. To get a camera now would make a mockery of all those camera-less, unrecorded expeditions. I also wonder, superstitiously, if the moment I possess a camera, the moment I buy a camera for the express purpose of recording my travels, I will suddenly cease travelling altogether, will never leave the house and will have to content myself with using my lightweight, automatic, highly portable camera to take pictures of the house I never leave.

In any case Laura has a lovely camera which is too heavy to take anywhere but because it is such a lovely camera she refuses to trade it in for a lightweight automatic which would take excellent pictures. Nine times out of ten we end up leaving the lovely camera behind and buying a disposable one which takes useless pictures. On this occasion, though, she was adamant about taking it.

'How are we going to take pictures of Lawrence without a camera?' she asked.

'I am a camera,' I said.

The train was as full as a rush-hour tube. Although we had arrived twenty minutes early we were the last to take our seats in our compartment. People were loading on bags and boxes as though it would be six months before we sighted a platform again. There was only just enough room for our bags in the luggage racks. Then a hefty man, the kind of man who, in books, is usually referred to as a 'fellow', came and pointed out to another, even heftier fellow that he was in the wrong seat. No, said the fellow who was already sitting, holding his ticket up for the other passenger's inspection, it was the right seat, and the right compartment . . . Wrong carriage! cried the standing man in vindication. They changed places and all the luggage was taken down again to extract the ousted fellow's suitcase and make room for his replacement's. Soon the corridor was so crowded that, to relieve congestion, it was necessary to take some more luggage into our compartment so that everything had to be taken down and loaded again, more rationally this time. We, the men, all stood up. Even if not lifting anything, we kept our arms raised, surrendering ourselves to the task.

A middle-aged couple were banging on the window trying to attract the attention of an adolescent boy in the corridor. He was wearing a Gauguin T-shirt and was embarrassed by the way his parents were making a big fuss about his leaving, waving and mouthing things at him through the window. He was more relieved than any of us when the air-conditioning hummed into life and, a few minutes later, punctual to the second, the train nudged out of Termini. Between us and the sky, the network of overhead wires and cables was so extensive it seemed merely the first stage of a project to put a sun roof over the whole of Italy. An alphabet of aerials stretched away over the roofs. Sheets and towels hung from every balcony. Washing hanging out to dry: that is the real national flag of Italy, emblem and proof of how the fabric of daily life endures.

Soon we were passing the truncated remains of an Ancient Roman viaduct; beyond that was a glimpse of the *autostrada* so that the essential trajectory of Roman history seemed a straight line, an unwavering determination to get somewhere else as quickly as possible. The mountains in the background were cut from the same cloth as the sky: a slightly darker shade, that was the only difference. Had we the capacity to analyse it there would almost certainly be a geology of the air as well as of rock.

The *controllore* came by, fining the young Gauguin because he had not stamped his ticket at the station: so *that's* what his parents were making such a fuss about. A new ruling this: unstamped, a ticket was now valid for three months which meant that it was advantageous to avoid stamping your ticket – hence the heavy fine for omitting to do so. Everyone felt sorry for the boy and the *controllore* relented, fining him the smallest possible amount. A great debate ensued about the injustice of this new ruling. The *controllore* went on checking tickets while all around him the debate – which in no way excluded him: just because he was charged with implementing the new rule did not mean he had to relinquish his right to be an Italian: *to join in* – became more energetic in spite of the fact that essentially everyone was in agreement. New laws are always being passed but they alter almost nothing. Their real purpose is, precisely, to engender debate, to give the people of Italy a chance to express a lively opposition to the state so unanimous that it actually creates a supportive atmosphere of unity and national well-being. Everyone feels the state is fleecing them, treating them unfairly, so that feeling cheated by the state – and finding some small ways of cheating the state – turns out to be the cement that binds the nation together. In this way the state is sacrificed to the idea of the nation. That's Italian history, in a nutshell.

The *controllore* rested his elbow on the door, put his foot up on the ashtray (not on the seat of course) so that he was now in the classic Italian discursive attitude: propped up, leaning in such a way as to suggest, as Italians always do, that discussion originated in the simple biological need to come to terms with the heat. Six months from now, he said, taking off his hat to emphasise that he was now speaking *ex cathedra*, he would be out of a job. The new ticket laws were the first step towards getting rid of *controllori*. So, the cult of rationalisation had come to Italy — and what a shame it was! In England we had completely absorbed the ethic of cost-efficiency. Cut costs — no matter what the cost! It comes easy to us. Even as we protest against a particular instance of it we accept, somewhere in our empirical English psyche, the principle that this is the way things must be. We can easily forsake the pleasures that come from that which is not strictly necessary — but in Italy, where life is devoted to making life that bit nicer, to providing an extra bit of sweetness in a *cornetto* (by their pastries ye shall know them!), it goes against the grain utterly. So what if the state is losing money? So what if it is more efficient to have some robotic fraud-proof ticket system? It is nice, fun, to have a handsome *controllore* come around like this in his pressed blue shirt, checking tickets and joining in the debate about his impending obsolescence.

The debate continued after the *controllore* had gone on to join in the debate in the next compartment. Not at all like being on a train in England where everyone is tacitly affronted by everyone else, terrified lest their legs touch those of the person opposite. England must be the only country in the world where you plonk yourself down next to someone in a train without saying a word, where the normal form of greeting is to keep your eyes fixed on the ground. Here, though, the six of us were perfectly at home in our little compartment. A railway compartment is actually the Italians' preferred version of the indoors. Ours was like a tiny piazza, a place to gather and discuss. The democratic ethos of the piazza-compartment is a product, like so much else in southern Italy, of the heat. None of the men was wearing a jacket. We were all in shirts or T-shirts. Madness to wear a tie on a day like this! Hierarchies are difficult to maintain without jackets. In shirts, people are practically equal – the only way to establish a jacket-less hierarchy is by turning the shirt into a uniform. Hence the frequency of military coups in South America, violent attempts to resist the levelling tendency of the shirt.

A drunk shoved open the door, asking for money. None was forthcoming and he threw some soiled abuse into the compartment. The man next to me, a waiter on the ferries, told him to watch his mouth. The drunk lurched out into the corridor and made the slightest, meanest gesture of a throat being cut – not one of those harmless piratical swipes across the whole of the throat, just a tiny slit to indicate that cutting open your neck would mean no more to him than nicking himself shaving. With that he was gone, snaking his way out into the corridor. A few minutes later, from the direction in which he had slithered, came the sound of commotion, or rather a sound over and above the normal commotion of the crowded corridor. The waiter was up on his feet and into the corridor instantly, hitching his jeans up over his stomach, a stomach which at that moment indicated neither sloth nor greed but a ballast of strength and fearlessness, immunity to slashing. He had blue eyes and dark, dark skin. His mere presence in the corridor subdued the throat-cutter who muttered off into the next carriage – first class, as it happened. Now he was really asking for trouble.

*

To travel is to eat. We were tucking into our lunch, which is to say Laura was munching crackers and I was eating bread and *pomodori*. These tomatoes tasted nothing like English tomatoes. They tasted *tomatoey*. I ate them one after another, the taste like a memory of childhood which actually turned out not to be a taste but a *smell* of taste, the reddening green smell – I had it exactly – of my Uncle Harry's greenhouse in Shurdington where the air ripened under glass. We offered our food to everyone in the compartment but no one accepted. We were the only ones eating. Everyone else was too busy talking about food to eat. They were all saving themselves for enormous meals tonight (especially the waiter from the ferries who had not seen his wife for two months). After lunch a consensus of silence fell on the compartment and a round of dozing took place.

I read *Sea and Sardinia*. More accurately, I read the first paragraph of *Sea and Sardinia* over and over until I felt sleepy. I loved the first sentence, its urgency of intention: 'Comes over one an absolute desire to move.' The sentence had ended, left, moved on, almost as soon as it had begun, while I, the diligent reader, was still checking that it had everything it needed to leave, to *be* a sentence. The whole of the first paragraph was like that, I thought to myself: a train that was moving out fractionally ahead of its appointed time, doors still ajar, leaving the reader running along after it, unsure where it was heading, but convinced of the need to climb aboard before it gathered too much momentum: 'Comes over one an absolute necessity to move. And what is more, to move in some particular direction. A double necessity then: to get on the move, and to know whither.' It was only with that quaint 'whither' that we had the chance to gather our senses and settle down comfortably in our seats. I love that first paragraph, I thought to myself, sleepily. I resolved to look at it more closely, to discuss it 'at length' in my study of Lawrence, the study I was going to Sicily to research. In Rome I'd had that idea of putting together an album of pictures of Lawrence. I still wanted to do that but now, after reading a paragraph of *Sea and Sardinia*, I also wanted to do a series of travel sketches of places Lawrence had been, an album of travel pictures, I thought, sleepily. Came over me an absolute desire to sleep . . . I opened my eyes once before falling asleep and saw that Laura had fallen asleep, in fact everyone in the compartment was sleeping so that it seemed I was standing guard, falling asleep when I was meant to be keeping watch.

I woke up, other people woke up or slept. I read, looked out of the window, slept, read, or dreamed I read and looked out of the window.

At Villa San Giovanni we sat on the train, waiting for the carriages to be loaded on to the ferry. We waited and sat and nothing happened. There was a strike, it turned out, by the men whose job it was to put the carriages on to the ferry. Italy is constantly in the grip of strikes like this, a very loose grip which causes no more than mild inconvenience. These strikes are hardly ever coordinated, never persist for any length of time and are unlikely to achieve their objective – if they even have one. Wild-cat strikes? The term is too fierce. Any disruption caused merges imperceptibly with the general disarray of Italian life. On this occasion it felt like we had arrived at the port at the moment when all relevant staff happened to be taking a protracted, unscheduled lunch break. No sense of a dispute, just a suspension of activity, an industrial siesta. We passengers also fell prey to this atmosphere of drowsiness. The boredom of the journey had turned to torpor. We sat around and waited, too sapped of energy and initiative even to be irritated or to find out what was going to happen.

We needed a leader and one emerged in the shape of a young soldier who had boarded the train at Napoli. He suggested we walk over to the commercial ferry port and catch a ferry there. We went with him, aimlessly, without urgency. A fat woman who was also a late recruit to the compartment said that wherever he was going, that was her destination too. The soldier dissuaded her from tagging along, explaining that it was a long walk and there were far too many stairs to climb. We left her in the compartment, fanning herself with a crossword magazine. We walked for ten minutes and boarded a ferry which left immediately.

The sea: you watch it for a while, lose interest, and then, because there is nothing else to look at, go back to watching it. It fills you with great thoughts which, leading nowhere and having nothing to focus on except the unfocused mass of the sea, dissolve into a vacancy which in turn, for want of any other defining characteristic, you feel content to term 'awe'. You lean on the rails, looking at the sea and the other ships whose passengers are leaning on the rails looking across at you, thinking about waving but somehow losing heart. The soldier said that the waters here in the Straits of Messina were very dangerous. A terrible undertow. Jump off the boat and you will be sucked under.

People who are separated from the mainland only by a thin strip of water often express pride and love of the sea in this way. Their version of 'Welcome' is always to point out that the sea is dangerous, treacherous, unfathomable, awash with currents and rip-tides which pull the unwary beneath the waves. Just because it is a small strip of water does not mean it is not a force to be reckoned with. That the sea is calm, safe, warm or good for bathing is nothing to take pride in; the sea must pose a threat. In England we do not need to make a meal of this because, on the one hand, the Atlantic is so obviously huge and daunting and, on the other, the Channel and the North Sea so blatantly unwelcoming, so obviously treacherous and harm-inducing, as to need no emphasis. But here, where the water was a lovely deep blue, attention had to be directed to the ills lurking below the surface. Maybe the waters *were* treacherous, I didn't know, but the soldier's remark actually had next to nothing to do with the sea, or at least the sea was being appealed to only as a metaphor, as a way of telling us something about the island it surrounded, about Sicily and the treacherous undertow of the Sicilian character.

We walked off the ferry without paying, 'English style', as our soldier-friend put it, intending no offence. None of us knew the way to the railway terminal.

'I'll ask,' said Laura who is always happy to ask.

'Don't ask,' said the soldier. 'Don't say anything. Let me do the talking.' Which was fine by me – except his idea of doing the talking involved saying nothing. After five minutes he hadn't said a word and we had made no progress.

'He won't ask the way and he won't let me ask the way,' said Laura. 'He has this code of silence thing.' Somehow we wound our wordless way to a taxi rank where we learned that the railway station was a good distance off. Of course it was a long way off. The nearest taxi rank is always the furthest distance from the place you want to go. A taxi was ready and waiting but before we climbed in Laura broke rank to ask how much it would cost. The driver went mad: did we doubt his honesty? How much would it be? It would be what it said on the meter. The soldier looked at her, vindicated. She had *asked* for it.

'It's like this in Sicily,' Laura whispered to me in the back of the taxi. 'You never know how they are going to react.' It was true. We were in one of those touchy 'respect' cultures where the smallest action can cause enormous offence, where people are relaxed to the point of torpor and, at the same time, ferociously uptight. They slumber and slumber and then, suddenly, they erupt. It probably has something to do with living in close proximity to a volcano. Best to keep quiet, like our soldier said. The driver took advantage of our silence to explain that some taxi-drivers would charge as much as 12,000 lire for the trip, but he put it on the meter, because he was honest.

'No,' interjected Laura, '*Non volevo dire*. I didn't mean to suggest—'

'What are you interrupting for?' interrupted the driver. 'He and I were talking – not you and me.' Oh yes, touchy as anything but still with a kind of slumbering good-naturedness beneath the fierceness, as if it were all just a joke.

Since the young soldier had helped us out I paid his share as well. 'Why did you do that?' he wanted to know, as if by paying for him I had offended him at least as much as I would have done by not offering to do so.

'*Quanto?*' I asked the taxi-driver.

'12,000 lire.'

The whole performance turned out to have been a pyrrhic one in that we now had to wait for our train – still stranded on the mainland – to catch up with us. Rather than wait we leapt on a local train and waved goodbye to the soldier with whom we had struck up this tense friendship.

Darkness fell on either side of our train. We were running along the coast, a ping-pong moon bouncing along beside us. The light in the compartment was yellowy old. We stood in the corridor, leaning on the window, seeing the sea. The train stopped as frequently as a bus. It was like a little dog, scurrying and panting, tireless. If we'd had time to dash around and look at the front of the locomotive it would surely have had eyes and a willing smile like Thomas the Tank Engine. While the train was moving we seemed to be the only passengers; the stations were deserted too but people got on and off at each stop as if they were using the carriages as a bridge to cross the tracks, stepping on to the right-hand side, getting off at the left and disappearing before the puppy train went panting on its way again, sniffing out the next station.

When we arrived at Taormina there was no sign of Ciccio, Laura's friend's mother's boyfriend, whose house in nearby Furci we were going to be staying in. We were both early and late. Later than the train was scheduled to arrive but earlier than the scheduled train was actually arriving. We phoned Ciccio who was engaged, then phoned Renata – Laura's friend's mother – who had just been on the phone to Ciccio who had come and gone and would return to meet our stranded train.

With half an hour to kill we looked for a place to have a beer. Opposite the station was what looked like a restaurant or, more exactly, like a living room in which there happened to be a great surplus of tables. A woman was watching a western dubbed into Italian. I'll say this for Italian TV: you're never more than a few channels away from a western. She was watching TV in that way of night porters the world over: they watch for hours but never become so absorbed in anything that they mind being interrupted. Given that there are a finite number of westerns and an infinite number of nights in which to watch them they figure that any gaps can be filled in later. To them each film is really no more than a segment of an epic ur-western spanning thousands if not millions of hours, offering a quantity of material so vast that it can never be edited into a finished form. The western thus takes the place of the great myths of antiquity: shifting glimpses of character and situations, variously recurring, but manifesting through the very fact of their myriad transformations, the existence of some stable, changeless order.

Laura asked if we could have just a drink, nothing to eat, and the woman said no, not just a drink. Then she gestured to us to sit down: she would bring us a drink. They are like that in Sicily, said Laura. Their instinct is to say 'no', but once they have established that a thing cannot be done they are happy to do it. In this way serving a bottle of beer takes on a near-miraculous quality. We drank our beer on the balcony of the deserted café, looking across the deserted road at the deserted station, engulfed, periodically, by the thunder of hooves and the whine of ricochets from the television. For the third or fourth time that day a strange, floaty indifference to everything came over me. Since this sensation was utterly unfamiliar and not at all unpleasant I decided that, if experienced again, I would refer to it as contentment.

Ciccio arrived just as our train pulled in. He was stocky, dapper (rare for a Sicilian) and tanned to his bones from fifty years of sun. Had they remained still for any length of time his eyes would have been kind; as it was he looked kind of anxious. He had a perfect, firm handshake, the sort that suggested that the handshake originated here in the south and was then exported north and west. I wondered: *did* the handshake originate, as I had once read (in a Fantastic Four comic) as a gesture of trust, a way of demonstrating that you had no weapon in your hand? Or was it, from the outset, a compromise, enabling both parties to offer one hand in friendship while keeping the other free for protection, a way of establishing physical contact while maintaining the maximum possible distance? I felt Ciccio would know. There was knowledge in his handshake.

As soon as we had been introduced, Ciccio dashed off to reassure Renata (who had been worrying about a botched rendezvous) that all was well. I folded myself into the back of Ciccio's small car, sharing the back seat with a cash register. It made the normal meter used in a taxi seem rather paltry, cheap. It was Ciccio's business, Laura explained. He sold and repaired cash registers.

We wound our way up to Taormina which looked like the most beautiful place imaginable: coves and headlands, sea glittering in the moonlight, lovely old buildings and restaurants. Had we come on holiday we would not have been disappointed at this moment. All the accumulated worry as to whether Taormina had been a good choice would have been dispelled, we would have put our arms around each other and exchanged glances full of love and decisions vindicated. Even in the midst of this realisation, however, part of me was thanking God that we were *not* on holiday, not playing that game with its stakes that are so low and so high. Ciccio parked and then called Renata from a passing payphone. This time Laura had a word and then we moved on.

To a fine restaurant with a magnificently deserted terrace overlooking the bay. Down below but still part of the same restaurant was another terrace, crowded, overlooking the bay. We had entered the hierarchical topography of tourism where everything, if it has any value, must be overlooking something else. Anything not overlooking something is to be looked down on. The lower terrace was less formal than the upper terrace – so formal, in fact, that there were no people in it – and so we walked down there. The waiter showed us to a table with a view overlooking the bay but Ciccio insisted on a better one, one with an even better view overlooking the bay. A second waiter took our order and a third brought our beer. They all knew Ciccio . We had our beer, Ciccio and I, but there was no sign of Laura's wine. 'Hey Franco,' said Ciccio, addressing a fourth waiter. '*Portaci del vino*. We need to make a toast.' One way or another Ciccio was keeping the entire staff of the restaurant on their toes.

Because it was one of the few things I knew how to say in Italian, or any other language for that matter, I remarked on the deliciousness of the beer – whereupon Ciccio ordered two more even though we still had a third of a glass each. We were drinking *grandi* beers not *piccole* because to have ordered *piccole* would have suggested some failure of hospitality. The trouble with *grandi* beers, though, was that we couldn't drink them fast enough: after a few minutes they were warm as tea and so the table filled up with half-finished glasses of beer which stood there not as waste but as excess, as trophies of hospitality. It was the same with the antipasti. Once I'd eaten my plateful, I asked Ciccio, for want of anything better to say, if we could go up for seconds. We couldn't, strictly speaking, but Ciccio insisted that I have some more – insisted, rather, that the waiter bring us another tray of bits and pieces. I became wary of mentioning anything lest Ciccio took it upon himself – or on one of the waiters – to provide it. Not for the first time in my life I felt the slightly wearying, not to say utterly exhausting nature of this commitment to hospitality which was always a part of these respect-offence cultures. My own preference was for that busy urban version of hospitality where, if friends of a friend turn up, you have a quick drink at the neighbourhood bar, give them towels and a set of keys, show them how the sofa bed works, say 'Mi casa es su casa' and leave them to their own devices for the next four days.

Still, drinking these half *grandi* and lavishing hospitality appeared to be having a calming effect on Ciccio. He had not phoned Renata for twenty minutes – but what I had taken to be calm actually turned out to be the lull before the telephonic storm. A waiter arrived with a cordless phone: there was a call for Ciccio: Renata. They spoke for ten minutes. Then Laura had a chat – then, although I had never met Renata (who spoke no English), it was my turn. After that we were ready for another round so I handed her back to Ciccio. While he was talking Laura said she would love to open a hotel.

'Would you?'

'Well, not a hotel: a *pensione*. I'd take such pride keeping it clean,' she said. By now the phone had achieved a position of such unquestioned predominance over our lives in Sicily that by simple virtue of the fact that it had been conducted face to face, in person, this exchange had a quaint, not to say archaic air about it.

Eventually Ciccio got off the phone and gestured for the bill. I offered to pay – English-style, without really expecting to – but Ciccio was already out of his seat, on his way to settle up. On the way out he introduced me to the manager of the restaurant, a guy with curly hair, a little younger than me, smoking a cigar and wearing a gingham jacket which may or may not have been – it was a question of style – too big for him.

'Ciccio said you were writing an article about the restaurant,' he said.

'Well, about Taormina, generally,' I said, catching on that Ciccio had settled the bill Sicilian-style, by saying I was writing an article for the British Airways in-flight magazine, the kind of piece that would guarantee a queue of customers seven nights a week.

'This is nice restaurant, we have to have something like this, casual like this, but I have another restaurant, really good restaurant. A high-class restaurant where everything is special. You should go there. Is a special place. I think you would like.'

'Yes I'm sure I would,' I said, thinking that if I had an air mile for every time someone had told me I would like something that I felt pretty certain I would hate – for exactly the reason they claimed I would like it – I could have circumnavigated the globe by now. I took a card for the restaurant and a flyer for the disco that he also ran. Before we left, I promised, we would try out both the restaurant and the disco.

Once we were out of the restaurant Ciccio was able to relax totally, in the sense that he was able to head straight to a payphone and call Renata. When he was through talking to her he drove us to Furci where we would be staying. I asked why a red light on the dashboard was flashing.

'Is to tell me I am not wearing seat belt,' Ciccio said. An EU ruling meant that all new cars were fitted with this warning device. A stupid and dangerous idea, he thought. The flashing distracted and could make you crash. But there was someone he knew who was going to disconnect the wires so that he could ride in comfort without his seat belt and without this flashing light. Wouldn't it be easier just to wear the seat belt? I asked, but that was beside the point. The point was that there was a way around this edict. Italians delight in exercising their ingenuity for trivial ends. To use ingenuity for some loftier purpose is somehow to diminish it. The more pointless the end the more vividly the means of achieving it is displayed. The further south you travel, the more extreme this tendency becomes. The ingenuity of the Romans, for example, is as nothing compared to that of the Neapolitans. Ciccio even knew someone who sold T-shirts with a diagonal black band printed across the chest so that the police would be deceived into thinking you were wearing your seat belt.

Furci, we saw the next morning, was a miserable little town with reinforced concrete rods sprouting from unfinished buildings that, for reasons of tax, had no chance of being completed. Ciccio had got up early and so we waited for a bus to take us back into Taormina, passing the time by watching a group of boys rough-housing. Boys in Sicily spend all their time larking around, rough-housing, teasing each other.

When they grow up and become men nothing changes – it's just that the pace of the larking around is scaled down until, by the time they are in their sixties, they do it sitting down, with hardly a word being spoken. Take this guy in a fat yellow T-shirt, waddling past on his bike. At thirteen he had been the fat boy who everyone teased; now, at thirty, he was a grown-up fat boy. His friends teased him and he cycled off, sulking, but then, in the forgiving way of fat boys who cannot bear to be on their own, he came back, ready for more.

On the corner of a street, in the shade, a woman was selling fish, calling out to passing motorists; an old man cycled past, selling oregano; a man shaving in a second-floor window conducted a prolonged conversation with a friend in the street: vivid instances of why – quite apart from the inherent musicality of the language – so many of the great opera singers have been Italian. Opera begins in the market where, over and above the simple demands of competition, of being able to attract customers' attention, stall holders have to convey the colour and taste of fruit in their voices. The man selling oregano, for example: he called out and the air was fragrant with oregano. His job was not to *sell* oregano but to fill the air with the sound of its scent. And while Italians are happy to be in close proximity to each other as we were on the train, they enjoy conversing from a great distance, or calling down the street to each other. The popularity of cellular phones is simply the technological manifestation of this inherited cultural trait.

As soon as we arrived in Taormina we began asking for Lawrence's house, the Villa Fontana Vecchia. No one knew of a *Villa* Fontana Vecchia but several people knew of a *Via*

Fontana Vecchia. We headed that way while Laura, now that we were no longer bound by the code of silence, stopped almost everyone to ask directions. It was as though we were not seeking guidance so much as canvassing local opinion as to the whereabouts of the Villa Fontana Vecchia. The results of such a survey confirmed our initial impression of Sicilians, for the typical response was to claim that there was no such place and then, once we looked suitably crestfallen, to direct us towards it. We wound our way there and began looking for the exact house. We saw a man reading *La Sicilia* in the distinctive way that Italians have of reading newspapers, especially the sports pages: he was *absorbed* in his reading, giving himself totally to the experience but with an expression of furrowed doubt etched into his face. Watching him, it seemed certain that reading the papers each morning had become a substitute for prayer. Reluctant to disturb him in his devotions we spoke to a woman with a limp who thought it might be the first house on the corner. A lovely old place, it turned out, which happened to be for rent. I decided then and there that I would rent it for six months in order to write my book because it was such a clear example of serendipity that the house Lawrence had lived in should be available to rent. The problem was that there was no way of confirming whether or not it was the right house. We asked another woman with an even more pronounced limp (they are great limpers, the Sicilians) who shook her head and said it was definitely not the house of Lawrence, it was her son-in-law's house.

We walked on and the Via Fontana Vecchia turned into Via David Herbert Lawrence. Ah! We were on the right track. It seemed a shame, though, that it wasn't called Via

Lorenzo which would have fitted in better with the other street names. Laura took my photo – with a newly bought disposable camera: having lugged the Nikon to Sicily, she had left it back in vile Furci – beneath the sign because that was the only way we could think of commemorating this discovery. We asked a man with a walking stick if he knew the house. He replied eagerly, as expected: men with walking sticks are always pleased to give directions: the act of raising the stick and pointing imparts to them something of the character of a prophet. Lawrence's house was the big place, quite a way off, on the right, the place with mustard-coloured walls. We plodded along the road that clung to the hillside. The sun lurched in and out of clouds, bougainvillaea dulled and burst into purple flame. The road had curled in such a way that we were now behind the houses pointed out by the prophet, and it was impossible to tell which one he had singled out.

'A common part of literary pilgrimage,' I said as we walked on, 'is that you often don't know which house you're meant to be visiting. In a sense it doesn't make any difference but it's very difficult to return home unless you have absolute proof that you've been to the right place. Hence the need, I conclude, for a plaque on the wall: to free us from doubt.'

We walked on. A man was opening his garage and Laura began to ask him about *la casa dello scrittore inglese* . . .

'*Si, si,*' he interrupted. '*È quella là.*' The pink one. On the other side of the road, approached from a gate at our level but actually perched up on the next contour line – everything in Taormina is perched on everything else. The top floor was painted pink. There were three green shutters, all drawn, and a long, very narrow terrace with black iron railings. The floor below was pale cream, also with a long terrace and three arched Norman windows of a kind often seen in Sicily (I'd never seen them before). To the left, painted yellow, was what looked like an annex or extension. A steep line of steps led down from the house to the locked gate at our level. Laura walked off to see if there was another entrance while I contemplated the house. Laura came back a few minutes later and I followed her up the road which took us behind the house. There were some roadworks going on and the whole area had a Moscow smell of petrol about it. It was obvious now that there were two apartments: the yellow annex and the main house, on the wall of which was a plaque:

D. H. Lawrence
English Author
11.9.1885 – 2.3.1930
Lived Here
1920 – 1923

We had found it. We stood silently. I knew this moment well from previous literary pilgrimages: you look and look and try to summon up feelings which don't exist. You try saying a mantra to yourself, 'D. H. Lawrence lived here.' You say, 'I am standing in the place he stood, seeing the things he saw . . .', but nothing changes, everything remains exactly the same: a road, a house with sky above it and the sea glinting in the distance.

We walked by the side of the house, peered over the fence. It was three in the afternoon, and if there was anyone in the house they were asleep. The only thing to do was to come back later. As we left we saw an old shoe lying on the low wall surrounding the house.

'Do you think this was Lorenzo's shoe?' said Laura. We were true pilgrims now, desperate for relics.

After our expedition to the Villa Fontana Vecchia which was both successful and abortive it was a relief to revert again to some recognisable, easily identifiable feelings: tourist weariness, a longing to be in a hotel, to sleep between sharp white sheets. It was too far to head back to vile Furci and so we had to kill time in a café. We took a cappuccino and then strolled to another café where we took a Coca-Cola, trying to recoup our energy, bored already by the prettiness around us. Forced into tourist mode, we sipped our Cokes and watched the other tourists go by: Italians who always went to Italy for their holidays, Americans who didn't know a word of Italian, who wore clothes which aspired to some constantly surpassed ideal of hideousness, who looked at gift shops selling nothing but rubbish, shops specialising in things no one in their right mind would ever want to buy. Thank God we were only on a little work-related jaunt, a research trip of sorts, and could leave whenever we wanted and go home. It would have been terrible to have come on a charter, to be condemned to two weeks' holidaying. Holidays are for people who work whereas we, who worked for ourselves, the last thing we needed was a holiday. For those who set off every day to an office or factory or shop, a holiday might be a nice relief but for us, who passed our time as we pleased, a holiday was an unthinkable burden. I had envied them sometimes, those in work, those with jobs. Especially on a Friday night when, relieved that it was over for another week, they could down tools and look forward to two days of uninterrupted idleness – until the thought of Monday began to intrude so that by Sunday afternoon all they could think of was getting to bed early, not doing anything that might jeopardise their return to the grindstone. Not now though. At this moment both sides of the deal – work and the holidays funded by work – seemed equally intolerable. Sitting here in Taormina, it was *my* life that I loved because it meant I didn't have to take holidays, didn't have to be a tourist even though at the moment I was feeling this exultant emotion I *was* a tourist, handing over money, paying for time to pass. I thought of Ciccio and his cash register business. I admired the purity of it: selling the means by which people reckoned up their profit. The only way to have got nearer to pure money-making would have been to manufacture the banknotes themselves. And what a perfect spot to work this particular hustle! In a town like this, where tourists came precisely to *spend* money, where every one of the dozens of sandwich bars and restaurants was pulling in money hand over fist, what product could be more in demand than a cash register? The cash registers of Taormina were ringing all day as people killed time, bought useless souvenirs, ate dinners and bought cappuccini to recover from their stroll-fatigue.

We paid for our Cokes, strolled down to the Greek amphitheatre and then strolled back into town, strolling ourselves into a state first of stroll-weariness and then stroll-exhaustion which was more exhausting than anything suffered in a forced march across Dartmoor in a blizzard. We collapsed into a café and then made our weary way back to Lorenzo's house.

It was six-thirty now, the men doing the roadworks were stowing away their tools for the night. I envied them their feeling of work-tiredness that was so different to our own stroll-fatigue, envied them their feeling of satisfaction and relief now that the working day was over. I even envied their arriving at work tomorrow morning, unlocking their hut and finding everything as they had left it the night before and doing a day's work in the tree-shadowed sun.

One of the workers knew the man who lived in what I had taken to be the annex of Lorenzo's house. He knocked on the door and introduced us to a middle-aged woman who listened patiently and showed us in – and immediately we saw that the two apartments were actually one. She introduced us to a man who had just got off the phone: Salvatore Galeano. The whole place was modernised twenty-five years ago, he explained, showing us around, but Lawrence's desk was still there. And his sofa. He introduced us to his mother who was sitting on a sofa – not Lawrence's sofa, another one. His mother was in her nineties now, Salvatore explained, but when she was a little girl she had delivered the post to Lawrence.

We went out on to the balcony: a lovely view of the bay, the sea and the sky. We looked at the view. That is exactly what we did; we did not look at the sea and the sky, we looked at the view. Laura took some photos of Salvatore and me together and then we began making our departure. As we were leaving, Salvatore said that someone else had come here about Lawrence. Ernest Weekly? No, Kinkead-Weekes, Professor Kinkead-Weekes had been here. Ah yes, Professor Kinkead-Weekes, I know him, I said, hoping, by this harmless fib (I knew *of* him), to lend myself a little credibility. By saying names in this way, people like Salvatore vouch for their own authority, their own suitability as custodians of a place, and this is why I too said, 'Ah, yes, I know him.' It was all perfectly understandable but it was impossible to imagine anyone saying that *I* had been here or anywhere else as a way of boosting their own credibility.

And it was not surprising, I reflected when we were out in the street again, for I had not asked Salvatore's mother anything. Even though she had known Lawrence I had said nothing to her except '*Buongiorno*,' which should have been '*Buonasera*'. How nice it would have been, how authoritative, if she had said, 'Mr Lawrence he was very nice, *molto simpatico*,' something like that. Spoken by a woman who had actually known him this otherwise unexceptional observation would have carried more weight than anything I had ever read about Lawrence in dozens of memoirs. This was as near to Lawrence as I was ever likely to get and I hadn't asked her anything, partly because she was old and tired and I was too respectful, but mainly because it had simply not occurred to me to ask her anything and now it was too late.

That night, as a gesture of appreciation, we invited Ciccio to dinner at the restaurant of his choice. A sea-food restaurant, as it turned out. Not a great choice from my point of view since sea-food is vile filth which I will eat under no circumstances. My favourite foods are all variants of bread, food you can chow down with no effort, without even a knife and fork, food that requires virtually no preparation and little expenditure of money or energy. At the other extreme there is food that you have to fiddle around with, food that comes in shells that you have to prise open, food that you have to prepare for hours and pick the bones out of and pay for through the nose: sea-food in short, and here we were in a sea-food restaurant. The first course arrived: not any old sea-food (i.e. not simply inedible) but the *ultimate* sea-food (i.e. there was actually nothing *to* eat): sea urchins, blackened conker shells with a tiny strip of (presumably) slimy, salty, orange gristle in the middle. A great delicacy, no doubt, in the tacit sense that delicacy is always employed: revolting filth that requires the greatest care in preparation otherwise you'll spend the next week crapping squid ink. Needless to say, as with all this revolting, salty-tasting crap, it is, allegedly, a great aphrodisiac.

'What's it like?' I asked out of politeness, crunching a *grissino* stick.

'You know when you were little and you jumped in the sea, and water went up your nose?' said Laura. 'It tastes like that. Only it doesn't burn.'

Ciccio and Laura crunched through a couple of plates of these blackened conker shells. As always happens with sea-food the detritus was way in excess of what little bits there were to eat and soon the table was piled high with urchin shells. What next? I wondered. Ah mussels, of course. I hate anything that comes in shells and this meal was going to be nothing but shell – shell and, if I was lucky, bones. By now I was desperately hungry and since although I will not eat sea-food I can eat fish – at a push – I helped myself to a portion of the fish that Ciccio had ordered for us all. I hadn't asked what kind of fish it was but I recognised it as soon as I had had my first mouthful: a bone fish, a fish so full of little white bones that you had to pick and inspect, sift and sort through every forkful to make sure you didn't choke – and after a while that demanded more concentration than it was worth so I just left it on my plate.

At that point, a low point for me, a friend of Ciccio's arrived bearing the bag of stuff we were to take back to Renata. He shook hands, handed over the bag and left. In the bag were cartons of Prozac: boxes and boxes of Prozac. The delivery of this consignment was clearly a relief to Ciccio and he was now able to get down to the serious business of the evening: phoning Renata. The waiter brought a cordless phone, Ciccio dialled and was immediately submerged in conversation. I had realised some time ago that Ciccio's phone bills were fairly heavy but now I saw that his acquaintances also bore part of the punishing cost of his relationship with Renata. After a surprisingly short time, however, he hung up.

'She's calling back,' he explained, unstrapping his watch and putting it on the table in front of him as if to say: right, now we're going to have a *real* phone call. After thirty seconds, though, she had still not called back and so he tried her again. Engaged. He lit a cigarette and tried again. Engaged. They had reached telephonic gridlock; both lines were engaged constantly because they were both trying to call each other. Drawing deeply on his cigarette, Ciccio mustered all his willpower and let the phone sit there unused. It rang and Ciccio snatched it up. It was Renata and she was close to hysteria. Why hadn't he called? The whole scene was like a government health warning for the adverse side-effects of Prozac. On the other hand what would she have been like without Prozac? Dead possibly, whereupon Telecom Italia would either suffer a major reduction in turnover or, alternatively, would have been free to liberate a good part of its network for more urgent matters than this mad romance.

At the end of the evening I settled the bill, still hoping,

even as I handed over my wad of lire, that Ciccio would either offer to pay or tell the owner that I was writing an article on his restaurant. We left the restaurant and Ciccio drove us back to vile Furci. We drove as if our lives depended on it, as if our lives didn't depend on it. We overtook everything in sight but, since other people were overtaking *us*, then — by the Italian law of highway moderation — we were driving perfectly safely.

I was looking forward to sitting on the train for eight or nine hours, reading Sea and Sardinia, thinking about Lawrence and Sicily, not budging from my seat. Instead, once we got to Villa San Giovanni, it was the train that refused to budge. More precisely, it budged a bit, shunting back and forth a few metres each way to hook up extra carriages from the ferry. The train extended itself by two carriages at a time until it was half a mile long. While all this was going on I hung out of the door, brake-man-style, looking out across the rails and the empty freights towards the blue Straits of Messina and, beyond that, Sicily. When the train was ready the doors shut and . . . we stayed where we were for another half an hour. Then the air-conditioning came on and . . . we stayed where we were for a while longer.

    This proved to be only the first instalment in a series of setbacks. Later, as we headed out of Napoli, there was a crash and my window shattered. An explosion of glass. We threw ourselves to the far side of the compartment which was full of screaming. Something had hit the window, shattering it, but, we saw now, the window was intact even though it had shattered. The double laminate had saved us: the outside pane had smashed but the inner one had held. A guard came running and the train pulled in at the next station, Aversa. A rock, he said, or a brick. It happens all the time. Boys gather on the bridges and hurl rocks and bricks at trains: a popular hobby in Napoli. Last year five people were killed.

'*Non è una buona idea*,' said the fat man sitting next to me, '*sedersi vicino al finestrino a Napoli.*'

A team of railway officials began digging out the remains of the window. We got off the train, milled around and got back on again. I took the same seat as before, aware now that there was only a single pane between me and the rock-strewn world outside. Everything proceeded smoothly until the intercom pinged into life and the guard asked if there was a doctor on the train. If there was a doctor on board could he go immediately to the back of the train because there was a medical emergency. We heard no more about it but at the next station the train made another unscheduled stop. At the far end of the platform, a stretcher was waiting.

'Whatever next?' said my plump neighbour as the train rolled on again.

Next, the guard announced that due to '*una interruzione fatale*' up ahead the train would have to stop at the next station, Cisterna. For how long? Everyone piled out of the train to find out, to mill around. Information was gleaned and passed on. The fat man from our compartment proved an invaluable source of information. By now I was into the spirit of the journey, hoping for even more catastrophic developments. I was happy to mill around in Cisterna with the evening sun angling over the station buildings. Especially since I now had the opportunity to do what was utterly forbidden in England: to walk across the tracks. I was not the only one to enjoy this. One group of passengers actually went and *sat* on the rails. Soon everyone was scampering across the tracks on some flimsy pretext or other. The delay also provided an excellent opportunity for the use of cellular phones: up and down the platform people were dialling home, postponing dinner. *Gelati* were bought and licked. A football was produced and a brief game of head tennis ensued. Someone began singing: a jokey song, Laura explained, about the love of a *controllore* for a beautiful passenger. Essentially, everyone took the opportunity to act like Italians. This is what Italians love to do more than anything: to act like Italians. They never tire of it! Day in, day out! Young boys, teenage girls, middle-aged mothers, even old men in their eighties – especially old men in their eighties! – they all love acting like Italians.

Laura asked if I could go up into the cab of the locomotive. The driver said it was not allowed but then, since nothing in Italy is utterly forbidden, he relented and Laura took a picture of me at the controls. Next she asked the guard to pose for a photo next to me so that our fellow passengers would be in no doubt that this was what the *inglesi* loved more than anything: to be treated like thirteen-year-olds. We were getting a lot of photos out of the trip back but it was difficult to imagine anyone collecting and poring over them the way I had done with pictures of Lawrence.

We milled around some more. Then, suddenly, the whistle! Back on the train! Back on the train! We were on our way again – as far as the next stop, where we got off once more and milled around again until the guard got the order to proceed.

We pulled into Termini five hours late. I had no

complaints. It had been such fun, getting on and off the train like the escaping POWs in *Von Ryan's Express*. The hours of mild catastrophe, of milling around and posing for photographs, had engendered a lovely spirit among the passengers, especially between the people in our compartment. On the platform Laura and I shook hands with them all, affectionately, and in the right spirit. In a way I wished that we were still in transit, were heading for some more distant, hindrance-littered destination so that we could all remain together. I was sorry to leave them.

I was in a strange state when we got back to Rome, to the apartment, to the home that was not my home. I found myself wondering about the trip to Sicily, about the absence of whatever feeling it was that I'd expected to have at the Fontana Vecchia, even though I hadn't known what that feeling was meant to be. I thought about an earlier trip I'd made, to Eastwood, that had played a decisive part in simultaneously making me want to write a study of Lawrence and in making me doubt that I ever would. I looked through the notes I had made and was surprised by the way so few of them were even about Eastwood. Laura had an interpreting job which took her out of town for a few days and I sat in the apartment in Rome, feeling sad, I suppose, missing my parents, thinking about Eastwood, about England, about Cheltenham and Algiers.

I had driven there, to the Lawrence country – north of Shakespeare's county, south of the Brontë country, bang in the middle of motorway country – from Gloucestershire (Dyer country) in December. Two hours of motorway weather: Contraflow Showers, Lanes Merge Squalls, Delays

Possible Drizzle. For several miles, just south of Birmingham, signs warned that there was 'No Hard Shoulder'. This seemed inaccurate: there were six lanes of hard shoulder but no motorway. Cars were triple-parked in both directions. I'd hoped there might be time to stop off at Ikea near one of the Birmingham exits but with the traffic jammed solid that looked increasingly unlikely. Probably the hold-up was caused by people heading to and from Ikea. Ikea had become so successful that, while still functioning as a retail outlet, it was also a museum. People visited these furniture hypermarkets as theme parks devoted to the Ikea Experience just as they would sample the Industrial Experience at Ironbridge, or anything else from the Experiential repertory of Heritage Britain. The difference was that at Ikea you could buy the experience as it was happening, before it became history; you could experience history as it was being made, take it home in flat-packs and install it yourself. Faced with the choice I was half tempted to abandon the Lawrence Experience in favour of the Ikea Experience: it's a recurring problem this urge to abandon what I've set out to do in favour of something else, not because this other option is more enjoyable but simply *because* it is something else. It's something I have half a mind to address – not just in this book, but now, immediately, even though this ambition is itself symptomatic of the condition it seeks to diagnose, a diversion from the task I'd originally set myself – whatever that was. In this instance, en route to Eastwood, a trip to Ikea was a particularly pointless diversion since I didn't have a home to put any furniture in. For the moment I was stuck with the Traffic Experience.

On either side of the motorway was a strip of grey-green countryside and then, just out of sight, another six-lane motorway: the countryside as hard shoulder. In the 1960s cities sprawled until they joined in conurbations; now motorways are following suit: since there is no longer anywhere for them to go they expand sideways, they merge. No need to travel in England any more: just wait for everything to merge.

It was almost midday by the time I merged into Eastwood. I was too irritable from the drive to go straight into the D. H. Lawrence Birthplace Museum and Gift Shop so I ordered a calming cup of tea in the White Peacock Café.

'Mug or cup?'

'Cup please,' I said, thinking that I could have said 'I said "cup".' I said cup because I have never enjoyed tea from a mug – and, for that matter, only rarely from a cup. Basically I don't like tea but what else is there? Life is really no more than a search for a hot drink one likes. Compared with cold drinks (beer, fruit juices, sodas, varieties of mineral water) there is a dearth of hot drinks, I thought to myself, sipping my cup of – as it happened – rather nice tea in the White Peacock Café. There was another customer in the café, smoking. I said, 'Hi,' and he grunted back. I could see him looking at me, thinking I was another of those Lawrence tourists come to visit the Lawrence Museum. For my part, I too was thinking: I am behaving exactly like someone who has come to visit the D. H. Lawrence Birthplace Museum. Impossible to pass oneself off as anything else. Why else would I be drinking tea in the White Peacock Café? Why else would I be in Eastwood?

The café was heated by a two-bar electric fire with wood surround, plastic coals and a corrugated backscreen, flickeringly suggestive of flame. A song by The Who came on the radio, taking me back down the vista of the years...

When I was twelve, we moved from our (end) terrace house to a semi-detached place on the corner of the Shurdington Road, five miles from the village where my father was born. The new house had a real (i.e. electric) fire; in the old house we had had coal fires. Some days in the old house, in November or January, I came home from school to find the living room filled with smoke. If the wind was blowing in a certain direction, or if the logs were damp, the living room would be smoky, my mother would be sitting there, waiting for me to come home from school. Winter. Dark already at four-thirty. A smoky room, my mother sitting there, my mother who is old now, who is getting older every day as she sits in the back room of the semi we moved to when I was twelve.

She loves to do jigsaws. We did them when I was a child and she still makes them now, on the same sheet of hardboard that my father cut for us thirty years ago. We sorted out the side pieces and made a hollow, unstable frame, then filled in the middle. (For years my father worked in a factory; even at home, in matters of carpentry, he was a conscientious craftsman. My mother too was diligent and careful in everything she did. Perhaps it was inevitable, then, that we should approach our jigsaws in a methodical not to say semi-industrial spirit. Work had entered into every facet of my parents' lives; even their leisure had some of the qualities of labour.) We allowed ourselves to consult the image on the box: quaysides usually, or lakes reflecting (confusingly) blue skies, the yellow leaves of surrounding trees. I liked action scenes from popular TV series like *Ripcord* (parachutists in freefall: hundreds of pieces of uniform sky) but my mother preferred images from nature which, with the exception of those taken in spring, summer or winter, were overwhelmingly autumnal in mood. Other people make jigsaws in different ways, imposing different rules (no looking at the box), granting themselves other freedoms (start where you like), but we always started with the edge. One, which we made several times, was an illustrated map of the British Isles with a curving blue edge of sea. For once we reversed our usual method: we started in the middle and worked our way outwards to the coast, to the sea. I remember it clearly, that jig-map, but I cannot see it as clearly as I remember it. Many famous places were illustrated but I can picture only the three we started out from: a Highland piper, Jodrell Bank, Stonehenge. (There was no plan to frame this book, to hold it in shape. I started in the middle with one or two images and am working my way outwards, towards an edge that is still to be made.) My mother still does jigsaws and she also loves to do crosswords, whole magazines of them. She is probably doing one now, just as she was doing one when I returned home from Eastwood that day, sitting by the fire in her red sweater, blue slacks and glasses. I sat with her for a while and she asked me for help with some clues. I grunted answers, usually 'I don't know.' To help her – the equivalent of using the image on the jigsaw box – she had an old reference book called *Words* on her lap. She sat by the fire, consulting *Words*, while my father, who has never seen the point of doing jigsaws or of reading, watched telly, the volume turned high because he is slightly deaf. Upstairs were all my books, a few on shelves, most in boxes, waiting for a permanent address.

The bells in Piazza Santa Maria in Trastevere tolled quarter to one – the longest sequence of bells: twelve long, three short. At the White Peacock Café a clock struck midday. I left and walked over to the Lawrence Museum. There was very little Lawrentiana in the gift shop window: teddy bears, mainly, and Christmas gifts. The house at 8a Victoria Street had been restored and refurbished to reflect 'the lifestyle of the working-class of Victorian times, and the early childhood of Lawrence himself'.

The parlour was oppressive, dark, a far cry from the light, Scandinavian interiors of Ikea. On one wall a framed square of tapestry made 'Home Sweet Home' seem like a curse. The room was dominated by the fireplace and fireguard which were painted black, coal-colour. Everything about the interior suggested that homes aspired to the appearance of mines – which in a sense they did. Instead of the earth weighing down on the galleries there was the great weight of dark sky pressing down. The town was a narrow seam burrowed out between earth and sky. Even the vernacular of this architecture is oppressive: skullery, parlour, hob . . . Heavy words: dark, sooty. The closed-in feeling of houses like this has nothing to do with cosiness. Everything has to be kept at bay (hence, perhaps, *bay windows*): dirt, weather, debts, the outside. This spirit lives on into the present day. Leaving the Lawrence Museum to follow the Blue Line Trail around Eastwood, the visitor will find the gates of many houses sporting signs like 'Beware of the Dog: Enter at Your Own Risk' or 'No Hawkers, No Salesmen, No Religious People'. Beyond these warnings, for the benefit of anyone familiar enough to ignore them, there is usually a mat saying 'Welcome'.

Upstairs from the parlour was a bedroom which looked like someone had died in it a century ago or the day before yesterday, whichever was the longer. Off-white, death-coloured night-dresses were spread on the bed which looked like it was designed to die in; either for dying in or giving birth in, ideally both at the same time. In a room like this rest seems a species of grief. Museum installations always have a touch of death about them. Houses have to live; they cannot be embalmed. This one died a natural death and then, after it had fallen into disuse, after it had decomposed, they tried to bring it back to life again but succeeded only in embalming it in death.

I moved quickly upstairs, experiencing that familiar urge to hurry through the part of the visit that should have detained me, the part that drew me to the place in the first instance. In another upstairs room, the ceiling was bedecked with bright plastic leaves to indicate – presumably – proximity to Sherwood Forest. In the centre of the floor, inscribed with the initials D.H.L., the author's travelling trunk occupied pride of place. The travelling trunk had become a piece of site-specific sculpture. You walked around it. The one thing you would not want to do with a trunk like this is travel with it. Luggage was something that interested me, a theme I'd contemplated exploring in my study: its evolution and development, the matrix of requirements, function and limitations (of weight and size) that go to make up a particular item. It wasn't a problem for Lawrence; back then there were legions of porters to lug around your trunks, no matter how unwieldy.

In the room next door a video gave an account of Lawrence and Eastwood. It opened with that northern brass band music which sounds like it marched to its own funeral more than a century ago, music whose every note is a lamentation for *its* having become extinct. Except extinction no longer means 'no longer in existence'. Plenty of extinct things are still around. Brass bands, for example: they're still going strong even though they are extinct; even though they're extinct they're still going strong. The video stressed that Eastwood and its environs was the 'country of Lawrence's heart'. He attended the Beauvale Board School, but, the commentary conceded, 'by all accounts hated' it, just as he hated the 'sordid and hideous' squares of purpose-built miners' dwellings. It was odd sitting there, watching this video about the man who seemed to hate so many things about the town that was now seeking not simply to honour him but to re-claim him as a local author.

Tired of looking through my notes, I walked across the Tiber to the Piazza Farnese. Some boys were playing football exactly as if they were playing for Inter or Roma: fouling, time-wasting, diving, appealing to the crowd at the beautiful injustice of the game.

It was a relief to be outside, to leave the Lawrence Birthplace and Museum, to step out of the dismal interior and into the different dismalness of the outside. A gang of lads were hoofing a football down the street. I followed the Blue Line Trail, a blue line painted on the pavement, linking 'the Birthplace with the three other houses [Lawrence] lived in and eight other Lawrence-related sites' (not counting the Lawrence Snackery, Lawrencetown Car Sales or the Lawrence Veterinary Surgery). Several places were not on the itinerary, like the Beauvale School and the British School where Lawrence taught for a while. 'Both buildings,' the video explained, 'were demolished in 1971 to make way for a new supermarket.' There you have it: attempts at conservation take place in the midst of the ongoing culture of ruination that is contemporary England. This is the heritage effect in a nutshell: protecting the odd pocket of wilderness or preserving the occasional building of historical interest, is actually a license to trash everywhere else. Not that Eastwood is worth preserving. The Blue Line Trail is a nice idea but there is no getting away from the fact that Eastwood is an ugly little town in an ugly little county. The countryside around Nottingham seemed beautiful to Lawrence, the mines an aberration, 'an accident in the landscape'. Yet the real crime of nineteenth-century industrialism seemed to him 'the condemning of the workers to ugliness, ugliness, ugliness: meanness and formless and ugly surroundings, ugly ideals, ugly religion, ugly hopes, ugly love, ugly clothes, ugly furniture, ugly houses, ugly relationships between workers and employers'. These days we scarcely even notice ugliness. We notice its absence. In the face of this pervasive ugliness the workers, according to Lawrence, hungered for beauty. What was the piano, often found in colliers' homes, 'but a blind reaching out for beauty'?

Three or four times a year we went to stay with my grandparents in Shropshire. My grandfather was a farm labourer, my grandmother smoked. That is all I remember of her: her smell and her cough. First she smoked and then she died of smoking, coughing herself to death in the bedroom above the room that no one knew what to call except the room with the piano in it. Never the piano room or the music room, but the room with the piano, conceding by this strange locution that the piano was not at home there. There were sheets of depressing music on the piano but no one could play it. I bashed away at the keys without enjoyment: it wasn't just that I had no aptitude for the piano or that there was no one around to teach me how to play: that piano had no music in it. So the only sound in the room was the noise of my grandmother coughing upstairs. She was dying of lung cancer but no one wanted to say the word cancer. Instead, to make things seem less hopeless, my parents said she had TB, the illness Lawrence could not bring himself to name, to acknowledge. He preferred to talk about trouble with his bronchials, pneumonia, flu – anything rather than tuberculosis.

The Blue Line Trail led to Walker Street, to the third of the four houses where the Lawrences lived. In a way it's quite appropriate, this trail. Lawrence loved to give directions. His letters are full of instructions to visiting friends on how to reach him at the various places he and Frieda were staying. From Florence, in December 1926, he wrote to Rolf Gardiner, directing him through his past, providing the Birthplace Museum with its main theme. There is no passage of Lawrence's writing that I love more than this one where the actual countryside changes in the process of composition into the semi-mythical Lawrence country.

> If you're in those parts again, go to Eastwood, where I was born, and lived for my first 21 years. Go to Walker St. – and stand in front of the third house – and look across at Crich on the left, Underwood in front – High Park Woods and Annesley on the right: I lived in that house from the age of 6 to 18, and I know that view better than any in the world. – Then walk down the fields

to the Breach, and in the corner house facing the stile I lived from 1 to 6. – And walk up Engine Lane, over the level crossing at Moorgreen pit, along till you come to the highway (the Alfreton Rd) – turn to the left, towards Underwood, and go till you come to the lodge gate by the reservoir – go through the gate, and up the drive to the next gate, and continue on the *footpath* just below the drive on the left – on through the wood to Felley Mill. When you've crossed the brook, turn to the right (the *White Peacock* farm) through Felley Mill gate, and go up the footpath to Annesley. Or better still, turn to the right, uphill, *before* you descend to the brook, and go on uphill, up the rough deserted pasture – on past Annesley kennels – long empty – on to Annesley again. – That's the country of my heart. – From the hills, if you look across at Underwood wood, you'll see a tiny red farm on the edge of the wood – That was Miriam's farm – where I got my first incentive to write. – I'll go with you there some day.

I stood there later the same day, outside the house on Walker Street, looking at council houses and satellite dishes, Spender pylons. Insofar as the word suggested something pleasing to the eye, it scarcely merited being described as a view. The pavement was grey with cold, the sky was pavement grey. It would have come as no surprise to find that in the local dialect there was a single expression for 'it's getting light' and 'it's getting dark'. If the sky was supposed to serve as a conduit for light then it was no longer working. It turned up on time each day but there was never anything doing. Skies have their history too, remember, and this one was still recovering from the bruising it took in the last century.

It was getting on for two. Soon it would be night and soon after that it would be Christmas. Then it would be January, and so on. Christ, I thought, how I would hate to live here. I'd rather live anywhere than here, I thought, even though there were plenty of worse places to live. During the miners' strike in the early 1980s it was said that the closure of collieries would tear the heart out of communities. As long as there is a video shop and an all-night garage, places get along just fine after the heart has been ripped out of them. The idea of community is appealed to as a way of registering how bad things have become. It is the word on everybody's lips when teenagers beat to death the deaf pensioner next door. That's when 'the local community is united in grief'. Otherwise 'community' is invoked only to lament its having passed. Better to get rid of it once and for all and take up the American idea of neighbourhood. Even if they live in the midst of it some people are always excluded, or can choose to exclude themselves, from the community. Everyone who lives in a neighbourhood belongs to it, is part of it. The principle is geographical, not demographic. The only way to opt out of a neighbourhood is to move out, as Lawrence did.

In a way, though, it was difficult to imagine a more fitting tribute to Lawrence than present-day Eastwood. Whingeing about the ugliness of Eastwood is somehow to wish that all writers grew up in Knole Castle. Lawrence grew up in this ugly little town and the best monument to him is its ugliness. It is even better than his own suggestion: 'Pull down my native village to the last brick,' he wrote in his late essay 'Nottingham and the Mining Countryside', 'and make an absolute clean start.' Except there are no clean starts, in architecture or anything else. Anything new is likely to be worse than what was there before. Going back to what we had before seems a better idea than starting over. Knock down tower blocks and build slums. Re-create Victorian Eastwood with decent plumbing and central heating. Still, I liked the idea of some radical Lawrence fanatics from the anarcho fringe of the heritage movement, insisting that the only way to reclaim him for good was to take him at his word and raze Eastwood to the ground.

A few years before going to Eastwood I had travelled to Algiers to read Albert Camus's 'Nuptials' and 'Summer' on site. It was an absurd expedition, like going to England hoping to find the London of Dickens. Predictably, nothing of the culture celebrated by Camus survived. Slowly and systematically Algiers had been transformed: from Paris to Stockwell. Camus said that if man needs bread and housing 'he also needs pure beauty which is the bread of his heart', but in Algiers necessity had ousted beauty. I remembered that line of Camus's in Eastwood, amid the ugliness that led Lawrence to admonish, with characteristic vehemence, that 'the human soul needs actual beauty even more than bread'. Lawrence and Camus: the miner's son, and the man whose mother had to ask a neighbour to read the telex informing her that her son had won the Nobel Prize.

After the Algerian War of Independence all the street names were changed and written only in Arabic. I took a taxi to Belcourt, the area of Algiers where Albert lived with his widowed mother until his mid-teens. The house at 93 Rue de Lyon (now Rue Belouizdad Mohammed) was a two-storey place with a small balcony overlooking the street, exactly as described in *L'Étranger* when Mersault whiles [away a] Sunday after his mother's funeral. Below were a dr[y cleaner's] and a watchmaker's. There was no sign or plaque. <u>The only thing to do, once I had arrived there, was to leave.</u> So what was the point in coming? At the time I didn't know, but in Rome, thinking about these trips – to Taormina, Algiers and Eastwood – the point seemed simple: this was where Camus had lived and I had gone there because he had lived there, just as I had gone to Taormina, to Eastwood. If Camus hadn't lived in Algiers I would not have gone to Algiers.

Wondering if it was worth it, I drove from Eastwood out beyond Brindsley and Underwood, vaguely in search of the ruins of the Haggs farm, home of Jessie Chambers, the Miriam of *Sons and Lovers*.

I couldn't find the farm but I stopped the car and looked across the fields, taking in that grazing English countryside I have never cared for: mud, tractor marks, hedgerows, scrubby land, brambles. A scene which generated its own weather, which dragged the sky down to its own level. A cowscape without cows. A BSE landscape. Farm weather: everything damp and giving off a dank sense that it had never dried out, would never dry out except in recollection, except in memory. The preferred nest of any bird in this part of the world was an old tyre. I picked up one of these tyres, propped near a gate which was itself leaning against the hedge for support. Water sloshed out from the tyre, water that had been lying there for a hundred and fifty years, before the tyre was even invented. The puddles by the roadside offered no reflection: the water was too old for that, was no longer sensitive to light. There was no wind: it was so still you wondered how the trees dispensed with their leaves. Did these trees ever have leaves, or did they just grow like that? Every now and then there was a break of birds from one bare tree to the next. The sky was moving towards rain. I felt cramped, hemmed-in, as if I were still indoors: a desolate, wall-less version of the indoors where the sky was a low, damp ceiling that leaked. It was not just the rain. The sea was seeping up through the foundations, coming through the earth.

In 1928 Lawrence replied excitedly to a letter from Jessie's brother, David, declaring that 'Whatever I forget I shall never forget the Haggs . . . whatever else I am I am somewhere still the same Bert who rushed with such joy to the Haggs.' A few months earlier, following a visit from his sister Emily, he had written: 'I am not really "our Bert". Come to that, I never was.'

I had often puzzled over the contradiction contained within these rival claims but as I stood in the drizzle, in the proximity of a place I had been unable to find, had not really looked for, it was obvious that they were both true, that they actually depended on each other for their truth. Taken on their own, individually, both would have been false; the truth lay in the contradiction.

On my next-to-last day in Algeria I travelled to the Roman ruins at Tipasa, fifty miles along the coast. As we began the long curve and haul out of the city, rain spotted the windshield. Difficult not to take the weather personally and on this day, when it was so important that the sun shined, I thought of Camus's own return to Tipasa: 'walking through the lonely and rain-soaked countryside', trying to find the strength 'which helps me to accept what exists once I have recognised that I cannot change it'. Not like me. I can't accept anything, *especially* things I am powerless to change. The only things I can accept are those that I do have the power to change. This, I suppose, is the opposite of wisdom.

We drove through mountains and then out along a dull coast road. We passed half-finished buildings, the inverted roots of reinforcing rods sprouting from concrete columns: the opposite of ruins: a premonition of vile Furci. Then, ten minutes from Tipasa, the clouds were rinsed blue and the sky began to clear. Shadows cast by thin trees yawned and stretched themselves awake. That is the thing about autumn in Algiers: even when it is cloudy there is the promise of sun.

By the time I entered the ruins the sky was blue-gold, stretched taut over the crouched hump of the Chenoua mountains. The ruins were perched right on the edge of the sea: truncated columns, dusty blue-prints of the past. The sea was sea-coloured, the heat had a cold edge to it. I walked through the remnants of ancientness until, close to the cliffs, I came to a brown headstone, shoulder-high, two feet wide. On it, in thin letters, was scratched:

> JE COMPRENDS ICI CE
> QU'ON APPELLE GLOIRE
> LE DROIT D'AIMER SANS
> MESURE ALBERT CAMUS

The monument was erected by friends of Camus after his death. Since then his name had been vandalised. The weather-worn inscription from 'Nuptials at Tipasa' was already difficult to read. Thirty years from now the words will have been wiped clean by the sun and the sea that inspired them. There was a hollow boom of surf as if some massive object had been chucked into the sea. Waves surfed in on themselves. The horizon was a blue extinction of clouds.

If my trip had a goal then I had reached it. More than anything else it was Camus's two essays evoking 'the great free love of nature and the sea' at Tipasa that made me come to Algeria. What I hadn't realised then and only understood later, in Rome, was that there was another, self-interested motive for travelling to Algiers and Eastwood: I came to these places, to Camus's and Lawrence's places, like Tess to the D'Urbervilles: *to claim kin with them*, to be guided by them.

I drove back to Cheltenham, glad of the motorways that had ruined the countryside, glad of the car that smudged the air, back to my parents' house on the semi-detached estate on the edge of town that had played its part in ruining the Cotswolds. I took a detour, past the house in Fairfield Walk where I was born, where my mother used to wait for me to return from school in that smoky room. Like Lawrence's mother, she was proud of the fact that we had an *end* terrace. There had been a simple hierarchy of domestic architecture then: terrace, semi-, detached. We moved into a semi-detached house, partly, I think to consolidate my status as a grammar-school boy. Most of the people at grammar school lived in semis. Now the cramped terraced house is worth more than the semi we moved into as part of our move up in the world. These days we *aspire* to terraced housing. A few doors along from our old house a place was for sale. I had half a mind to call the estate agent: perhaps there would be some doomed fulfilment in ending up in the same street where I was born.

I also thought of knocking on the door of our old house, explaining that I was born there, that I lived there until I was eleven, and wanted to look around. I abandoned the idea as soon as I'd thought of it. Houses have no loyalty. We can live in a place ten years and within a fortnight of moving out it is as if we have never been there. It may still bear the scars of our occupancy, of our botched attempts at DIY, but it vacates itself of our memory as soon as the new people move their stuff in. We want houses to reciprocate our feelings of loss but, like the rectangle of unfaded paint where a favourite mirror once hung, they give us nothing to reflect upon. Often in films someone goes to a house where he once spent happier times and, slowly, the screen is filled with laughing. This convention works so powerfully precisely because, in life, it is not like that. It testifies to the strength of our longing: we want houses to be haunted. They never are.

When I last saw him my father said he was glad to leave our old house because of the view from the front-room window which was actually a view of nothing except other houses. When we were selling the house someone came to see it and said, looking out the window: 'Not very pretty is it?' It wasn't. Better than the view from Walker Street as it now is, not a patch on the view Lawrence evoked – and nothing like the view from the window of Laura's apartment where I sat looking through the notes I had made in Eastwood, where I am actually sitting, months later, writing this. What could be more lovely? A jumble of fifteenth-century buildings so close together that – Calvino has suggested – a bird might think that these roofs were the surface of the world, that the streets and alleys were canyons, cracks in the red-tiled crust of the earth. Sheets hung out to dry, pairs of jeans running on thin air. Balconies overflowing with plants. Just visible in the distance, the dome of Saint Peter's. And over all of this, a sky of Camus-blue . . .

When Laura came back from her assignment we spent our afternoons under that sky, sunbathing on the roof, and our evenings hanging out at the Calisto. I had a few articles to write, simple things, but time-consuming enough to make me lose what little momentum I had built up on my study of Lawrence. It was because these articles were so simple, in fact, that I stalled on the Lawrence book. What was the point flogging my guts out writing a study of Lawrence that no one would want to read when I could bang out articles that paid extremely well and took only a fraction of the effort? Especially since Lawrence himself felt the same way: 'I feel I never want to write another book. What's the good! I can eke out a living on stories and little articles, that don't cost a tithe of the output a book costs. Why write novels any more!' He expressed similar sentiments on numerous occasions; at one point he reckoned he was losing his 'will to write altogether', meaning, on this occasion, that he no longer even felt like writing letters. I was so heartened by this that my interest in writing about Lawrence revived to the extent that I started in on Rilke's letters again. By now, I had persuaded myself, reading Rilke was part and parcel of working on my study of Lawrence. *'Il faut travailler, rien que travailler.'* It was a shame, Rilke thought, that we had so many seductive memories of idleness; if only we had 'work-memories' then perhaps, without recourse to compulsion or discipline, it would be possible to find 'natural contentment' in work, in 'that one thing which nothing else touches'. The worst thing, for Rilke, was that he had these two kinds of memory, both these impulses, in himself: a longing, on the one hand, to devote himself to art and, on the other, to set up a simple shop with 'no thought for the morrow'. Laura's version of this normal life was – and still is – to run a *pensione*. She had mentioned it in Taormina and several times since coming back she had talked about the pride she would take in keeping it clean. My version of this was to live in England and watch telly. The ideal situation for us both would have been to have watched a series about an Italian *pensione* on telly. Rilke did more or less the same thing, reconciling these impulses by making his vision of contentment the subject of a poem, 'Evening Meal'. More broadly, this tension between life and work remained one of the dominant preoccupations of his life – and work. 'Either happiness or art,' he declared, struggling to assimilate the example of Rodin. 'All the great men have let their lives get overgrown like an old path and have carried everything into their art. Their life is stunted like an organ they no longer use.' Yeats offered the same choice: perfection of the man or the work.

For some writers there has scarcely been any friction between the demands of the life and the demands of the work. John Updike arranged his circumstances to his liking fairly early on and then simply got on with his writing, book after book, day after day. At the opposite extreme there was John Berger who only managed such extreme changes in his writing by corresponding changes in how and where he lived. For Rilke, too, the real work was to organise his existence, to will himself a life that would create the ideal conditions in which to work. Allowing life to atrophy so that he might work was itself a way of enhancing his life – even though the demands this made on his life, on his life-capacity, were immense and unremitting. To make *things* he had constantly to re-make himself: '*Du mußt dein Leben ändern*' ('i.e. find a different princess to live off' was Larkin's sardonic gloss).

And to what end, this subordination of life to work? There may be an 'ancient enmity between our daily life and the great work' but this relationship is more fluid, more complex, than the aphoristic formula from 'Requiem for a Friend' allows. 'For one human being to love another human being: that,' Rilke conceded, 'is perhaps the most difficult task that has been given to us, the ultimate final problem and proof, the work for which all other work is merely preparation.'

Lawrence was untroubled by any of this. All the work of his maturity was built on his relationship with Frieda. 'Fidelity to oneself means fidelity single and unchanging, to one other one.' His adult life begins with the unalterable fact of his marriage. As for work, he wrote when he felt like it, didn't when he didn't. Idleness seems to have held no attraction for him as a seductive ideal: the division between work and rest seems to have been as natural as that between sleeping and waking. Writing the novels took an enormous toll, obviously, but to Lawrence, the miner's son who had grown up amidst the ravages of gruelling physical labour, living by his pen was not such a bad option. He spent no time agonising over the rival claims of work and life because the two were inextricably bound together. 'I don't sacrifice myself for anything but I do devote myself to something.' And to what did he devote himself? To writing? No. To living ('not the work I shall produce, but the real Me I shall achieve, that is the consideration'). To say this is to reiterate one of the most hackneyed aspects of the Lawrence myth but it is difficult to improve upon, or at least his own version of it is: 'I *don't* think that to work is to live. Work is all right in proportion: but one wants to have a certain richness and satisfaction in oneself, which is more than anything produced. One wants to *be*.'

That was all very well but I had no richness and satisfaction in myself, more like a poverty and dissatisfaction. I had made progress on my study, that is, I had made progress in my mental preparation but now I had stalled. My lassitude was irritating me a good deal and this meant that Rome irritated me a good deal too. There had been several mornings when the Caffè Farnese had not had the *cornetti integrali* that I depended on for my breakfast. Without these *integrali* – more accurately *with* the disappointment of not having had my *integrali* – I found it difficult to get started on my work. I sulked, I went on a tacit strike as a protest against the Farnese and its undependable supply of *integrali*. I picked up books and put them down, thought about doing some writing and then did the washing-up instead. I recognised all these signs of unfocused anxiety and began to wonder if it might not be a good idea to move somewhere else to write my study of Lawrence. Laura's apartment should have been the perfect place to work but I couldn't get any work done there. I recognised *that* feeling too. Over the years I had come across several places that offered the ideal conditions to work. The room in Montepulciano, for example, with the lovely wooden bed and white sheets, the window gazing out over the Tuscan countryside, the terrace formed by what had once been a little bridge connecting our building to the one next door. Or the house in Lauzun with the room overlooking a field of wheat, facing west so that in the evenings the paper on the desk was bathed red. Or my apartment on Rue Popincourt with the floor-to-ceiling window from which you could see right down Rue de la Roquette, as far as the Bastille almost.

What they all had in common, these ideal places for working, was that I never got any work done in them. I would sit down at my desk and think to myself *What perfect conditions for working*, then I would look out at the sun smouldering over the wheat, or at the trees gathering the Tuscan light around themselves, or at the Parisians walking through the twilight and traffic of Rue de la Roquette, and I would write a few lines like 'If I look up from my desk I can see the sun smouldering over the wheat'; or 'Through my window: crowded twilight on the Rue de la Roquette'; and then, in order to make sure that what I was writing was capturing exactly the moment and mood, I would look up again at the sun smouldering over the flame-red wheat or the crowds moving through the neon twilight of Rue de la Roquette and add a few more words like 'flame-red' or 'neon', and then, in order to give myself over totally to the scene, would lay down my pen and simply gaze out at the scene, thinking that it was actually a waste to sit here writing when I could be looking and by looking – especially on Rue de la Roquette where the pedestrians hurrying home in the neon twilight would look up and see a figure at his desk, bathed in the yellow light of the anglepoise – actually become a part of the scene, whereas writing involved not an immersion in the actual scene but its opposite, a detachment from it. After a very short time I would grow bored by contemplating the scene, would leave my desk and go for a walk in the wheatfield sunset or leave my apartment and walk down to the Bastille so that I could become one of the people walking back through the neon twilight of the Rue de la Roquette, looking up at the empty desk, bathed in the light of the anglepoise . . .

When I thought of the ideal conditions for working, in other words, I looked at things from the perspective of someone not working, of someone on holiday, of a tourist in Taormina. I always had in mind the view that my desk would overlook, thereby overlooking the fact that the view from the desk is invisible when you are actually working, and forgetting that of the many genres of sentence I dislike there is none that I despise more than ones which proceed along the lines of 'If I look up from my desk . . .' The ideal conditions for working were actually the worst possible conditions for working.

And in any case maybe all this fuss about the conditions for working was irrelevant. After all, did it matter so much *where* you lived? The important thing, surely, was to find some little niche where you could work; to settle into a groove and get your work done. Logically, yes, but once, in north London, I had found myself walking along the road where Julian Barnes lived. I didn't see him but I knew that in one of these large, comfortable houses Julian Barnes was sitting at his desk, working, as he did every day. It seemed an intolerable waste of a life, *of a writer's life especially*, to sit at a desk in this nice, dull street in north London. It seemed, curiously, a betrayal of the idea of the writer. It made me think of a picture of Lawrence, sitting by a tree in the blazing afternoon, surrounded by the sizzle of cicadas, notebook on his knees, writing: an image of the ideal condition of the writer.

Or so it had appeared in memory. When I actually dug it out it turned out that there was no notebook on his knees. Lawrence is not writing, he is just sitting there: which is why, presumably, it is such an idyllic image of the writer.

He is wearing a white shirt, sitting with his back to a tree. (What kind of tree? Had he been looking at a photograph of someone else sitting there, Lawrence would have been able to identify it immediately. He was one of those writers who knew the names of trees.) Everything is still, but, sculpted by the absent wind, the branches record its passing. A hot, hot day. Lawrence sitting by the tree, the fingers of both hands laced together over his left knee. Schiele fingers. Thin wrists, thick trousers. Freshly laundered, pressed, his white shirt is full of the sun in which it has dried. Like the shirt of the prisoner facing execution in Goya's *The Third of May 1808*, it is the bright focus of all the light – and there is a *lot* of light – in the photograph.

Lawrence's jacket is rolled up beside him on the grass. The sleeves of his shirt are rolled down, buttoned around his bony wrists, lending a formal quality to the picture. By the 1920s photographs no longer required the interminable exposure times of the Victorian era (when heads and limbs had to be clamped in place to prevent blurring), but they were nearer to that unwieldy stage of photographic culture than to the Instamatic images of the post-war era. In early portraits, as part of the preparation for having a photograph taken, people focused their lives 'in the moment rather than hurrying past it'. Here, too, there is a strong sense of Lawrence *sitting* for a photograph. As far as formality is concerned the final touch is provided by the way that Lawrence's shirt is buttoned up to the collar. Why does that collar hold not just Lawrence's shirt but the photograph itself together?

Because even here, in the midst of this audible heat, Lawrence has to be careful to keep warm. He feels the cold, has to be careful not to catch a chill (the thick jacket is close to hand). His mother's concern for the sickly child – years of being told to keep warm, to keep his jacket on – have been internalised. By now, in the heat, it is second nature to cover up his skinniness, to keep himself warm.

His feet are invisible, buried in the grass, creating the impression – emphasised by the way that his body was surrounded by the trunk of the tree ('the tree's life penetrates my life, and my life the tree's') – that Lawrence is growing out of the ground. 'Thank God I am not free,' he wrote from Taos in 1922, 'any more than a rooted tree is free.' This line caused Larkin some astonishment. 'It is hard to see how he could have been less encumbered in the affairs of life,' he wrote from Leicester almost thirty years later. 'Put him down in salaried employment or with a growing family or an ageing one – why, he didn't even own a house & furniture!'

This is not strictly true: Lawrence *did* own some furniture (Brodsky was right: there is 'no life without furniture') , much of which he made himself. And while he may not have owned a house, the Lawrences' constant moving obliged them to keep *making* home. It is typical of Lawrence that, on the one hand, he became more and more anxious about finding a place to settle and, on the other, achieved the ideal condition of being at home anywhere: 'I feel a great stranger, but have got used to that feeling, and prefer it to feeling "homely". After all, one is a stranger, nowhere so hopelessly as at home.' That was from Taos in 1922; three years later the emphasis had changed: 'One can no longer say: I'm a stranger everywhere, only "everywhere I'm at home".'

He had found a home within himself and in what he did, in his *being*. Rilke had admired the same thing in Rodin who lived in a house that 'meant nothing to him' [Rodin] because 'deep within him he bore the darkness, peace and shelter of a house and he himself had become the sky above it and the wood around it and the distance and the great river that always flowed past'. Lawrence had likened himself to a rooted tree; sunk in himself, Rodin, according to Rilke, was 'fuller of sap than an old tree in autumn'. He had 'grown deep'. This idea, of being at home in yourself as a way of being at home in the world, was to receive its most exalted expression in the final lines of the last of the *Sonnets to Orpheus*:

> Whisper to the silent earth: I'm flowing.
> To the flashing water say: I am.

I'd torn the photo of Lawrence by the tree out of a biography published by the University of New Mexico Press. Before doing so I had tried to find where and when it was taken but there was no information. It was the only uncaptioned photo in the book. Had there been a caption I might have felt more reluctant about committing that small act of bibliographical vandalism. As it was, there had been no text to anchor the photo to the book, nothing to keep it in place. It seemed apposite that this, the only uncaptioned image in the book, was now free of the only context – the physical one of the book – available. If the bust made by Jo Davidson showed Lawrence what he would become in death, when – as suggested earlier – the loose pages of his life were bound and dated, then this picture showed Lawrence unbound, alive.

A photograph's meaning is bound up closely with its caption. As the photograph frames the subject, so the caption frames the photograph. Without a caption a photograph is not quite developed, its meaning not fixed. With a little research I could have found out – could still find out – where and when it was taken but I preferred, and prefer, not to: it seemed fitting that this photograph of Lawrence sitting there, 'happy as a cicada', should elude place and time. Like this it was a photo of Lawrence in the state evoked by Rilke in his sonnet; like this I *could* identify the tree: it is a photo of Lawrence sitting by a bho tree.

Buddha was sitting under a bho tree when he achieved enlightenment and in the spring of 1926 Lawrence told Brewster that he was 'convinced that every man needs a bho tree of some sort in his life. What ails us is, we have cut down all our bho trees . . . Still, here and there in the world a solitary bho tree must be standing . . . And I'm going to sit right down under one, to be American about it, when I come across one.'[1]

Another picture of Lawrence, the one I always hoped to come across in bookshops, the one that I had seen when I was seventeen, showed him – if I remember rightly – standing

---

[1] What Lawrence intended to sit under, Rilke, in the first of the *Duino Elegies*, was content merely to glimpse and speculate upon: 'Perhaps there remains for us some tree on a hillside . . .'

towards the edge of a vast horizontal landscape. Clouds streamed across the sky. I forget which book I saw it in all those years ago but I remember thinking that the caption – 'A fine wind is blowing the new direction of Time' – had been chosen so perfectly that the picture seemed less a photograph of Lawrence (a tiny figure in the corner, recognisable only by his beard) than an illustration of this line. At the time I did not know where it was from: a quotation from Lawrence, presumably, but beyond that I had no idea. I wanted to track that quotation down – or, to put it more passively and accurately, I hoped to come across it – and the prospect was intriguing precisely because there was nothing to go on. From the start, in other words, I read Lawrence in order to make sense of – to better understand – a photograph of him.

The urge to discover the source of this caption also explains my pleasure in reading Lawrence's letters in what might seem to be the ludicrously complete Cambridge edition. Or, to make the same point the opposite way, perhaps my pleasure in reading Lawrence's letters is the culmination of an urge, the first pulse of which was felt twenty years ago when I saw what I later discovered was a line from 'Song of a Man Who Has Come Through'. From that moment on, part of the incentive to read Lawrence was to discover the source of this line, to read it in the original, as it were, without quotation marks. I came across it in the Penguin *Selected Poems* (the edition that I still had with me in Rome, the one that I didn't take to Alonissos) but my satisfaction was qualified (or so it seems to me now) because everything in a 'Selected' format comes in tacit quotation marks: those provided by the editor's choice of material. When we read a 'selection' we are, so to speak, in the realm of massively extended quotation. When we read the author's work in definitive or collected editions, however, we are *there*: nothing comes between us and the writer (the often cumbersome editorial apparatus serves, paradoxically, to facilitate the intimacy between reader and writer). Like this I can read Lawrence *unquoted*.

'You mustn't look in my novel for that old stable ego of the character . . . the ordinary novel would trace the history of the diamond – but I say "diamond, what! This is carbon".' *Those* lines, even if we read them in the collected edition of Lawrence's letters, seem like a citation. Their true context is in a book about Lawrence – this one, for example! When we see them in Volume 2 of the *Collected Letters* it almost seems as if Lawrence lifted them from one of the hundreds of critical studies of him. And *so* much of my early reading of Lawrence came in quotation marks. At a very early stage 'doing' English became synonymous with reading criticism, most of it by academics. Go into any university bookshop and you will see stacks and stacks of books on Lawrence by academics. Such books form the basis of literary study in universities and none of them has anything to do with literature.

In my final year at university there was a great deal of fuss about course reform. Instead of ploughing through everything from *Beowulf* to Beckett, academics like Terry Eagleton were proposing a 'theory' option. I didn't know what theory was but it sounded radical and challenging. Within a few years 'theory', whatever it was, had achieved a position of dominance in English departments throughout Britain. Synoptic works of theory were pouring from the presses. Fifteen years down the line these texts still appear radical and challenging except in one or two details, namely that they are neither radical nor challenging. One Christmas when I was about ten my parents gave me a *Beryl the Peril* annual which included some of Beryl's answers to difficult exam questions. Asked to construct a sentence using the word 'discourse' she wrote '"Discourse is too hard for me," said the golfer.' How quaint! Twenty years on she would probably have no trouble coming up with a whole paper on 'The Self and its Others'. In no time at all theory had become more of an orthodoxy than the style of study it sought to overthrow. Any lecturer worth his weight in corduroy was fluent in discoursese, could signify-and-signified till the cows came home.

Hearing that I was 'working on Lawrence', an acquaintance lent me a book he thought I might find interesting: A Longman Critical Reader on Lawrence, edited by Peter Widdowson. I glanced at the contents page: old Eagleton was there, of course, together with some other state-of-the-fart theorists: Lydia Blanchard on 'Lawrence, Foucault and the Language of Sexuality' (in the section on 'Gender, Sexuality, Feminism'), Daniel J. Schneider on 'Alternatives to Logocentrism in D. H. Lawrence' (in the section featuring 'Post-Structuralist Turns'). I could feel myself getting angry and then I flicked through the introductory essay on 'Radical Indeterminacy: a post-modern Lawrence' and became angrier still. How could it have happened? How could these people with no feeling for literature have ended up *teaching* it, writing about it? I should have stopped there, should have avoided looking at any more, but I didn't because telling myself to stop always has the effect of urging me on. Instead, I kept looking at this group of wankers huddled in a circle, backs turned to the world so that no one would see them pulling each other off. Oh, it was too much, it was too stupid.

I threw the book across the room and then I tried to tear it up but it was too resilient. By now I was blazing mad. I thought about getting Widdowson's phone number and making threatening calls. Then I looked around for the means to destroy his vile, filthy book. In the end it took a whole box of matches and some risk of personal injury before I succeeded in deconstructing it.

I burned it in self-defence. It was the book or me because writing like that kills everything it touches. That is the hallmark of academic criticism: it kills everything it touches. Walk around a university campus and there is an almost palpable smell of death about the place because hundreds of academics are busy killing everything they touch. I recently met an academic who said that he taught German literature. I was aghast: to think, this man who had been in universities all his life was teaching Rilke. *Rilke!* Oh, it was too much to bear. You don't teach Rilke, I wanted to say, you kill Rilke! You turn him to dust and then you go off to conferences where dozens of other academic-morticians gather with the express intention of killing Rilke and turning him to dust. Then, as part of the cover-up, the conference papers are published, the dust is embalmed and before you know it literature is a vast graveyard of dust, a dustyard of graves. I was beside myself with indignation. I wanted to maim and harm this polite, well-meaning academic who, for all I knew, was a brilliant teacher who had turned on generations of students to the *Duino Elegies*. Still, I thought to myself the following morning when I had calmed down, the general point stands: how can you know anything about literature if all you've done is read books?

Now, criticism is an integral part of the literary tradition and academics can sometimes write excellent works of criticism but these are exceptional: the vast majority, the overwhelming majority of books by academics, especially books like that Longman Reader are *a crime against literature*. If you want to see how literature lives then you turn to writers, and see what they've said about each other, either in essays, reviews, in letters or journals – and in the works themselves. 'The best readings of art are art,' said George Steiner (an academic!); the great books add up to a tacit 'syllabus of enacted criticism'. This becomes explicit when poets write a poem about some great work of art – Auden's 'Musée des Beaux Arts' – or about another poet: Auden's elegy for Yeats, Brodsky's elegy for Auden, Heaney's elegy for Brodsky (the cleverly titled 'Audenesque'). In such instances the distinction between imaginative and critical writing disappears.

When it comes to reviews and essays in which writers address other writers and other books, on the other hand, it would seem that they are engaged in something indistinguishable from academic criticism. But this formal narrowing of difference in kind enhances the difference in spirit. Brodsky has gone through certain poems of Auden's with the finest of combs; Nabokov has subjected Pushkin to forensic scrutiny. The difference is that these works of Pushkin's and Auden's were not just studied: they were lived through in a way that is anathema to the academic...

Except this is nonsense of course. Scholars live their work too. Leon Edel – to take one example from hundreds – embraced Henry James's life and work as perilously intimately as any writer ever has. I withdraw that claim, it's ludicrous, it won't stand up to any kind of scrutiny. I withdraw it unconditionally – but I also want to let it stand, conditionally.

Scholarly work on the texts, on preparing lovely editions of Lawrence's letters is one thing but those critical studies that we read at university... Research! Research! The very word is like a bell, tolling the death and the imminent turning to dust of whichever poor sod is being researched. Spare me. Spare me the drudgery of systematic examinations and give me the lightning flashes of those wild books in which there is no attempt to cover the ground thoroughly or reasonably. While preparing to write *Etruscan Places* Lawrence thanked a friend for sending an authoritative book on the subject by Roland Fell who was

> very thorough in washing out once more the few rags of information we have concerning the Etruscans: but not a thing has he to say. It's really disheartening: I shall just have to start in and go ahead, and be damned to all authorities! There really is next to nothing to be said, *scientifically*, about the Etruscans. Must take the imaginative line.

That's why Lawrence is so exciting: he took the imaginative line in all his criticism, in the *Study of Thomas Hardy* or the *Studies in Classic American Literature*, or the 'Introduction to his Paintings'. Each of them is an electrical storm of ideas! Hit and miss, illuminating even when hopelessly wide of the mark ('the judgment may be all wrong: but this was the impression I got'). Bang! Crash! Lightning flash after lightning flash, searing, unpredictable, dangerous.

In truth I prefer these books to the novels which I have kept putting off re-reading. I re-read *The Rainbow* in Rome and I could have forced myself to re-read *Women in Love*, could have forced myself to sit down and peer at every page – or so I like to believe: who knows if, when it came to the crunch, I really had it in me? – but, I thought, why should I? Why should I re-read this book that I not only had no desire to re-read but which I actively wanted not to re-read. I had no desire to re-read *The Rainbow* but, unwilling to give myself the benefit of the doubt, sat down and re-read it, just to be on the safe side. I re-read the same copy that I had read first time around: part of the uniform Penguin editions of Lawrence with photographs on the cover (roosters or hens in this case) and, on the back, a sepia photo of Lawrence with beard (naturally) and centre parting. When I re-read *The Rainbow* I had thought I might discover, like a flower pressed between the pages, the dried remains of my younger self preserved within it. In the most literal sense I was there, the underlinings and annotations, made when we did the book at Oxford (i.e. when we read a load of dreary critical studies about it), were still there but in any kind of metaphorical sense – no, there was nothing, no traces of my earlier self, no memories released by the act of re-reading the same page that I had read years before one particular afternoon wherever and whenever that was.

My impressions of the book were more or less unaltered. It remained a book which I had no desire to re-read; as soon as I had finished re-reading *The Rainbow* it reverted to being what it was *before* I re-read it: a book which I had read and which I had no desire to re-re-read. It was a closed book: even when it was open and being re-read it was somehow still a closed book. As for *Women in Love*, I read it in my teens and, as far as I am concerned, it can stay read.

If we're being utterly frank, I don't want to re-read *any*

novels by Lawrence. And not only do I not want to *re*-read some of Lawrence's books I don't even want to *read* all of them. I want to keep some in reserve – I want to know that there are bits and pieces of Lawrence that are still out there, still fresh, waiting to be discovered (by me at least), waiting to be read for the first time.

In this respect I made a serious mistake in Rome, a mistake of such magnitude, in fact, as to jeopardise any chance of going on with – let alone completing – my study of Lawrence. From the start I'd known that I had to write my book as I went along. There are people who like to complete all the reading, all the research, and then, when they have read everything that there is to read, when they have attained complete mastery of the material, *then* and only then do they sit down and write it up. Not me. Once I know enough about a subject to begin writing about it I lose interest in it immediately. In the case of Lawrence I knew I'd have to make sure that I finished writing my book at exactly the moment that I had satisfied my curiosity, and to do this the writing had to lag fractionally behind the reading. Especially when it came to Lawrence's letters. The letters were Lawrence's life and I knew I had to ration my reading of them, not get too far ahead of myself. They were my main resource, a source so rich I knew I'd squander them if I just burrowed away at them from beginning to end. I knew that I could not be closer to Lawrence than I was while reading his letters for the first time. Ideally, if I were going to spend eighteen months writing my book about D. H. Lawrence I would be reading those letters for sixteen or even seventeen months, for a year at the very least.

But what did I do? I read them, all seven volumes, cover

to cover, in two months. It's my parents' fault. When I was a child they rationed out my sweets too slowly and so I grew up to be a gobbler. That's what I did with Lawrence's letters: I gobbled them all down and in no time at all there were none left, the bag was empty. I couldn't stop myself, couldn't help it. I loved reading them too much. I read Volume 2, then 3, then 5, then 4, then 6, then 1 (which I had no real interest in, whizzing through it in a day and a half). That left Volume 7. Whatever you do, I said to myself, keep Volume 7 in reserve: under no circumstances read Volume 7 because then you will have nothing left to read. It should have been relatively easy because there were so many other books to read — I could have re-read *Women in Love* (which I couldn't face re-reading), or one of the numerous critical books on Lawrence (which I had decided were a waste of anyone's time to read) or the poems or plays but instead I kept *glancing at* Volume 7, touching it, holding it, opening a few pages, reading the introduction. Finally I thought I would read just the first few letters even though I knew that reading the first few was exactly what I had to avoid because I would not be able to stop after three or four letters. After three or four I would keep reading another one or two until I had read so many that it would be pointless to stop reading the book and before I knew it I would have read all the Lawrence letters. And so the important thing was to avoid even opening the book: I knew it would be easier to avoid starting to read the book than it would be to stop reading the book once I had started. I knew all this but I opened it anyway, thinking to myself that I would read the first few letters. Which I did. But since these letters were pretty insignificant in themselves, harmless, I read one or two more which were also pretty innocuous and

I thought I would keep reading until I came to a significant letter and *then* stop. It went on like that until I realised with a shock that I was in danger of finishing all of Lawrence's letters. I read one after another and the more I read the less there were *to* read and although I knew part of the reason for reading the letters of Lawrence was to put off the moment when I had to write about him I also realised that by reading the letters like this, by failing to moderate my consumption of the letters, I was caught up in the gathering momentum of his death. I was running out of letters to read just as Lawrence was running out of life. The nearer I got to the end of the book the shorter and more insignificant the letters became, little gasps of anger where before there had been long, thousand-word rants, and so the pace of decline accelerated. Even insignificant communications – 'Blair has been kind as an angel to me. Here is £10 for housekeeping' – became something to cherish against the coming end.

And then, abruptly, there were no more letters. It was the end: oblivion. There were no more letters. If only, I found myself thinking, if only there had been Volumes 8, 9, 10 or 11. I had read four thousand pages of letters by Lawrence and I wanted thousands of pages more . . . I wanted them not to end. And yet, at the same time that I was wishing they would not come to an end, I was hurrying through these books because however much you are enjoying a book, however much you want it never to end, you are always eager for it *to* end. However much you are enjoying a book you are always flicking to the end, counting to see how many pages are left, looking forward to the time when you can put the book down and have done with it. At the back of our minds, however much we are enjoying a book, we come to the end of it and some little voice is always saying, 'Thank Christ for that!'

Still, better reading than writing. One of the reasons I was enjoying reading the Lawrence letters so much, and the main reason I wished that there were more Lawrence letters to read, was because they were a perfect excuse for not writing my book about Lawrence. Whereas now I had no choice, no choice at all.

It was a terrible prospect since although I had read the Lawrence letters and was therefore obliged to begin writing about Lawrence I had also read his letters in such a way that I was actually in no state to begin writing about Lawrence. Not only had I read them too fast, I'd also read them out of sequence, as they became available at the British Council Library in Rome, so that all sense of chronology, of development had been lost. One moment Lawrence was in New Mexico, the next he was eighteen months younger, in Italy, putting off going to America. If I had done it properly I would have read them sequentially and paced it so that my reading of the letters kept pace with the writing but now a huge six-volume gap had opened between my reading and my writing. I was like an out-of-condition athlete in a race who had lost touch with the front runners and the group in the middle: it was too much of a haul to get back in touch. I was out of the race, finished. The only alternative to giving up was to keep plodding round the track for the sake of finishing, grinding it out, metre by metre, page by page.

Not only had I read the Lawrence letters too fast and out of sequence, I had also failed to take notes. I had intended doing so as I went along, transcribing any particularly important passages and keeping a careful record of where these passages occurred, but I had been in such a hurry to gobble down the letters that, except on a few occasions, I had not done so. Not only that, I realised as I glanced back through the volumes of letters that I had already read, but there were many that, in my eagerness and impatience to get through all seven volumes, I had taken no notice of. The more I looked, the more letters there were that I had no recollection of. I could read the letters again because I had read them so badly the first time around. In fact, I realised with a sinking heart, I was practically obliged to re-read the Lawrence letters which I had longed to go on reading but which, now that I *had* to go on reading them, I wished to God I was shot of.

In no time at all, though, I was back under their spell. There were actually hundreds of letters which I had not read at all, which I saw for the first time as I re-read them. Like this one from November 1916 when, in the course of a letter to Kot, Lawrence remembered a time when he had seen an adder curled up in the spring sunshine, asleep. The snake was not aware of Lawrence's presence until he was very close and then 'she lifted her head like a queen to look' and moved away. 'She often comes into my mind, and I think I see her asleep in the sun, like a Princess of the fairy world. It is queer, the intimation of other worlds, which one catches.'

Queer, too, the intimation of future works which one catches so often in the letters. In this case the writing of the famous poem 'Snake' was still several years distant but here we have, as it were, a first draft of the experience which will later form the basis of the poem. This is one of the pleasures of the letters: one has the very first touch of a poem. It is like watching a fire and seeing the first lick of flame along a log:

you think it is about to catch but then it vanishes. You watch and wait for the flame to come back. It doesn't – and then, after you have stopped looking, the flame flickers back again and the log catches.

Lawrence began writing his greatest poem, 'The Ship of Death', in the autumn of 1929. According to Keith Sagar, the opening image of the poem –

> Now it is autumn and the falling fruit
> and the long journey towards oblivion

– was suggested by a visit to Rottach in late August when he noticed the 'apples on tall old apple-trees, dropping so suddenly'. But the first intimation of the poem actually comes as early as New Year's Eve, 1913, in a letter to Edward Garnett: 'it is just beginning to look a bit like autumn – acorns and olives falling, and vine leaves going yellow'. I *had* made a note of that, and of the occasion a few months later when I felt the rhythm of the image pulsing into life long, long before Lawrence began working on the poem: 'the apples blown down lie almost like green lights in the grass'. It was like a cadential draft of a poem that was nowhere near being written, and as I went through the letters for the second time I noticed more and more pre-echoes like this. As Sagar points out, the immediate source for the image of the ship of death was a 'little bronze' one he saw in Cerveteri in April 1927. Already by the summer of 1925, however, the opening image is redolent with the atmosphere of departure and journeying that will make up the poem's narrative: 'seems already a bit like autumn, and there is feeling of going away in the air'.

Who can say when a poem begins to stir, to germinate, in the soil of the writer's mind? There are certain experiences waiting to happen: like the snake at Lawrence's water trough, the poem is already there, waiting for him. The poem is waiting for circumstance to activate it, to occasion its being written.

As time goes by we drift away from the great texts, the finished works on which an author's reputation is built, towards the journals, diaries, letters, manuscripts, jottings. This is not simply because, as an author's stature grows posthumously, the fund of published texts becomes exhausted and we have to make do not only with previously unpublished or unfinished material but, increasingly, with matter that was never intended for publication. It is also because we want to get nearer to the man or woman who wrote these books, to his or her being. We crave an increasingly intimate relationship with the author, unmediated, in so far as possible, by the contrivances of art. A curious reversal takes place. The finished works serve as prologue to the jottings; the published book becomes a stage to be passed through – a draft – en route to the definitive pleasure of the notes, the fleeting impressions, the sketches, in which it had its origin.

In the case of Lawrence this process coincides with the gravitational pull of his work, which is always – another reversal – away from the work, back towards the circumstances of its composition, towards the man and his sensations. As is so often the case, it is Frieda who best captured this: 'Since Lawrence died, all these donkeys years already, he has grown and grown for me . . . To me his relationship, his bond with everything in creation was so amazing, no preconceived ideas, just a meeting between him and a creature, a tree, a cloud, anything. I called it love, but it was something else – *Bejahung* in German, "saying yes".'

This saying 'yes' – like Larkin's saying 'no' – is heard most clearly in Lawrence's letters. It is audible in the novels, too, of course, but it becomes more pronounced, more exposed, as we descend the traditional hierarchy of genre. In the novels the meeting between Lawrence and the world is mediated, inevitably, by Gudrun and Ursula, by the authorial representatives, by the demands of novelisation. Always, in the major works, the primary meeting is between Lawrence and the novel form which he is trying to mould, to recast in his own needs. What we want now, 'all these donkeys years' later, is Lawrence in the midst of his sensations. 'Whoever reads me will be in the thick of the scrimmage,' he wrote in January 1925, 'and if he doesn't like it – if he wants a safe seat in the audience – let him read somebody else.' In the novels we are in the scrimmage of art which, however apparently artless, will always be less of a scrimmage than the life unfolding in the letters. It is there, in the letters, that the scrimmage – the essence of Lawrence's art – is most nakedly revealed. Nor does it matter, in Lawrence's case as it does with some writers, if the prose of the letters is less honed, more error-prone, than in his published writing. Lawrence was, in some ways, a relatively careless writer, indifferent, or so he claimed, to the appearance of his words on the page. 'What do I care if "e" is somewhere upside down, or "g" comes from the wrong fount? I really don't.' Needless to say, this easy-going attitude to matters typographical did not stop him lambasting publishers for failing to pick up on exactly these kind of mitsakes: without this capacity for energetic self-contradiction there would be no scrimmage.

It is for this reason, I think, not simply because of his fame, that Lawrence's manuscripts became so sought after. His writing urges us back to its source, to the experience in which it originates. Ideally – and I am here trying to suggest the *direction* of an urge not necessarily an actual wish – we would have *met* Lawrence (in a way that even his admirers, surely, have no desire to have met E. M. Forster). Failing that we want the experience of reading him to be as intimate as possible; for the collector – I imagine – this means unmediated even by typesetting. Frieda had as sharp a sense of the possible commercial value of the *Lady Chatterley* manuscripts as anyone but she also understood and expressed perfectly the special poignancy of this intimacy: 'I enjoy looking at them,' she said, 'and reading them in the raw as it were.'

Some of Lawrence's books would have benefited from thorough, careful revision but what was essential about Lawrence – the qualities that made his writing identifiably Lawrentian – is always present at a draft stage. The improvements that come from redrafting are of relatively minor importance compared to the shock of his first encounter with the subject or incident he is addressing. In the elegy written shortly after his death Rebecca West explained how she felt unable to make the point that she wanted about Lawrence's work without recourse to her personal acquaintance with him (note again that familiar motion, from the work, back to the source, from the work to the man who made it). She met him, briefly, in Florence in the company of Norman Douglas who explained that it was Lawrence's habit to arrive in a place and immediately, before he was in any position to do so, to start banging out an article about it. Douglas and West knocked on the door of Lawrence's hotel room and there he was, fresh off the train, 'tapping out an article on the state of Florence at that moment without knowing enough about it to make his views of real value'. Later she realised that 'he was writing about the state of his own soul at that moment, which . . . he could render only in symbolic terms; and the city of Florence was as good a symbol as any other.'[1]

'I feel there is a curious grudge, or resentment against everything,' Lawrence observed, grudgingly, on arriving in New Mexico, 'almost in the very soil itself.'

Seven years earlier, in the autumn of 1915, Lawrence made a number of visits to Garsington Manor, the home of Ottoline Morrell. On 9 November, the day after his arrival, he wrote the first of several visionary accounts of his experiences there:

> When I drive across this country, with the autumn falling and rustling to pieces, I am so sad, for my country, for this great wave of civilisation, 2000 years, which is now collapsing, that it is hard to live. So much beauty and pathos of old things passing away and no new things coming: this house of the Ottolines – It is England – my God, it breaks my soul – this England, these shafted windows, the elm trees, the blue distance – the past, the great past, crumbling down, breaking down, not

---

[1] Lawrence himself said more or less the same thing in *Kangaroo*. The autobiographical figure Richard Lovat Somers 'wearied himself to death struggling with the problem of himself and calling it Australia'.

under the force of the coming buds but under the weight of many exhausted, lovely yellow leaves, that drift over the lawn and over the pond, like the soldiers, passing away, into winter and the darkness of winter – no, I can't bear it. For the winter stretches ahead, where all vision is lost and all memory dies out . . . I can't bear it: the past, the past, the falling, perishing crumbling past so great, so magnificent.

As soon as he returned to London he wrote to tell Ottoline how that visit would 'always be a sort of last vision of England to me, the beauty of England, the wonder of this terrible autumn: when we set the irises above the pond, in the stillness and the wetness'. By the end of the month he was back at Garsington again and from there he wrote another, related letter to his hostess:

So vivid a vision, everything so visually poignant, it is like that concentrated moment when a drowning man sees all his past crystallised into one jewel of recollection.
The slow, reluctant, pallid morning, unwillingly releasing its tarnished embellishment of gold, far off there, outside, beyond the shafted windows, beyond, over the forgotten, unseen country, that lies sunken in gloom below, whilst the dawn sluggishly bestirs itself, far off, beyond the window-shafts of stone, dark pillars, like bars, dark and unfathomed, set near me, before the reluctance of the far-off dawn:
the window-shafts, like pillars, like bars, the shallow Tudor arch looping over between them, looping the

darkness in a pure edge, in front of the far-off reluctance of the dawn:

Shafted, looped windows between the without and the within, the old house, the perfect old intervention of fitted stone, fitted perfectly about a silent soul, the soul that in drowning under this last wave of time looks out clear through the shafted windows to see the dawn of all dawns taking place, the England of all recollection rousing into being:

the wet lawn drizzled with brown sodden leaves; the feathery heap of the ilex tree; the garden-seat all wet and reminiscent:

between the ilex tree and the bare, purplish elms, a gleaming segment of all England, the dark plough-land and wan grass, and the blue, hazy heap of the distance, under the accomplished morning.

So the day has taken place, all the visionary business of the day. The young cattle stand in the straw of the stack yard, the sun gleams on their white fleece, the eye of Io, and the man with side-whiskers carries more yellow straw into the compound. The sun comes in all down one side, and above, in the sky, all the gables and the grey stone chimney-stacks are floating in pure dreams.

There is threshed wheat smouldering in the great barn, the fire of life; and the sound of the threshing machine, running, drumming . . .

It is an extraordinary letter, an extraordinary vision – or series of visions – of England: a synthesis in prose of Blake, Constable and Turner. Part of Lawrence's intention was to show his aristocratic friend how full of writing he was but there is also a sense of the words welling up in him unbidden. Each paragraph pulses into life from the seed of the preceding one; each paragraph offers an amended version of the same material; each version enters more deeply into the experience and, at the same time, advances it incrementally. It is like hearing alternate takes of a piece of music but, as these different versions unfold, so a narrative emerges: the narrative of his attempts to fix an experience that is vast, shifting, apocalyptic.

In the earlier letters England was lodged precisely within the confines of the aristocratic house. There is no acknowledgement of Eastwood – of his own experience and history – being a part of this essential England. In the last letter, however, the world 'beyond', 'that lies sunken in gloom' is acknowledged, distantly. At this stage in the letter the house is evoked in terms of the architecture of its own soul ('the perfect old intervention of fitted stone' etc.); the spirit of the house is talking but, as we move through successive variations, this 'vision of a drowning man' becomes Lawrence's own vision 'of all that I am, all I have become, and ceased to be. It is me, generations and generations of me, every complex, gleaming fibre of me, every lucid pang of my coming into being. And oh, my God, I cannot bear it.' Effectively, Lawrence imaginatively claims the house as his own. He fuses absolutely with the house and the surrounding landscape so that what is really coming to an end here – or what is coming to consummation – is Lawrence the *English* writer. It is not only the most vivid example imaginable of West's point, it also shows us – at a moment of supreme tension in Lawrence's life – the process at work, as it is happening.

Notes flare into writing, writing smoulders into notes, resulting in one of the most intense and revelatory passages Lawrence ever wrote.

If this book *aspires* to the condition of notes that is because, for me, Lawrence's prose is at its best when it comes closest to notes.

In *Sea and Sardinia*, for example, Lawrence *made* no notes during the ten-day trip but dashed off a book in a few weeks shortly afterwards. The lack of notes, in other words, accounts for the book's note-like immediacy. Notes taken at the time, on the move, and referred to later – as I referred later to the notes I had made in Eastwood – would have come between the experience and the writing. As it is, everything is written – rather than noted and then written – as experienced. The experience is created in the writing rather than re-created from notes. Reading it, you are drenched in a spray of ideas that never lets up. Impressions are experienced as ideas, ideas are glimpsed like fields through a train window, one after another. Opinions erupt into ideas, argument is conveyed as sensation, sensations are felt as argument. This immediacy is inscribed in the writing of the book. The transformation from 'notes' to 'prose' often takes place within the course of a sentence. We have to wait a long time for the pronoun that transforms the writing from diary-like jottings to finished prose. Sometimes it doesn't happen at all. Experience and sensation are rarely reined into shape until the last possible moment.

Would it be too silly – would it destroy any vestige of critical credibility this study might have – to claim that *Sea and Sardinia* is Lawrence's best book? Well it's my favourite at any rate ('the judgment may be all wrong: but this was the impression I got'), with *Studies in Classic American Literature*, *Twilight in Italy* and – if they count as a book – the posthumously published 'Last Poems' coming close behind. Best of all, though, are the letters: they show Lawrence at his most modern, his least dated. Unlike the thunderhead prose of the Garsington letters, Lawrence's later style of note-writing is unelaborated, spare. It is seen at its most minimal – so to speak – in the stunned letters dashed off soon after he arrived in Australia, a country he considered 'not so much new as non-existent':

> The land is here: sky high and blue and new, as if no one had ever taken a breath from it; and the air is new, strong, fresh as silver; and the land is terribly big and empty, still uninhabited . . . it is *too* new, you see: too vast. It needs hundreds of years yet before it can live. This is the land where the unborn souls, strange and not to be known, which shall be born in 500 years, live. A grey foreign spirit. And the people who are here, are not really here: only like ducks that swim on the surface of the pond: but the land has a 'fourth dimension' and the white people swim like shadows over the surface of it.

Bruce Chatwin doesn't even get *near* to that kind of responsiveness and suggestiveness in the three hundred pages of *The Songlines*.

'Have you noticed how often a writer's letters are superior to the rest of his work?' wonders Comtesse d'Arpajon in

Remembrance of Things Past. She had in mind Flaubert (though his name escaped her at the time). I tend not only to agree but to wonder if this remark might not be prophetic. Could my own preference for writers' — not just Lawrence's — notes and letters be part of a general, historical drift away from the novel? For Lawrence the novel was 'the one bright book of life', 'the highest form of human expression so far attained'. Nowadays most novels are copies of other novels but, for Lawrence, the novel still contained these massive potentialities. Marguerite Yourcenar offers an important qualification to this idea when, in her notes on the composition of *Memoirs of Hadrian* (a text of far greater interest, to me, than the novel to which it is appended), she writes that 'In our time the novel devours all other forms; one is almost forced to use it as a medium of expression.' No more. Increasingly, the process of novelisation goes hand in hand with a strait-jacketing of the material's expressive potential. One gets so weary watching authors' sensations and thoughts get novelised, set into the concrete of fiction, that perhaps it is best to avoid the novel as a medium of expression.

Of course good, even great, novels continue to be written but — as someone remarks every twenty years or so — the moment of the form's historical urgency has passed. Part of the excitement of reading Lawrence comes from our sense of how the potentialities of the form are being expanded, forced forwards. That feeling is now almost wholly absent from our reading of contemporary novels. If the form advances at all it is by increments, not by the great surges of the heyday of modernism.

Milan Kundera's faith in the novel is the equal of

Lawrence's but the logic of his *apologia* for the form actually carries him beyond it. Kundera takes inspiration from the unhindered exuberance of Rabelais and Sterne, before the compulsive realism of the nineteenth century. 'Their freedom of composition' set the young Kundera dreaming of 'creating a work in which the bridges and the filler have no reason to be and in which the novelist would never be forced – for the sake of form and its dictates – to stray by even a single line from what he cares about, what fascinates him'. Kundera duly achieved this in his own fictions, the famous novels 'in the form of variations'. In his 'Notes Inspired by *The Sleepwalkers*', meanwhile, Kundera paid tribute to Broch who demonstrated the need for 'a new art of the *specifically novelistic essay*'. Novels like *Immortality* are full of 'inquiring, hypothetical' or aphoristic essays like this but compared with these, my favourite passages, I found myself indifferent to Kundera's characters. After reading *Immortality* what I wanted from Kundera was a novel composed entirely of essays, stripped of the last rind of novelisation. Kundera duly obliged. His next book, *Testaments Betrayed*, provided all the pleasures – i.e. all the distractions – of his novels with, so to speak, none of the distractions of character and situation. By Kundera's own logic this 'essay in nine parts' – more accurately, a series of variations in the form of an essay – which has dispensed entirely with the trappings of novelisation, actually represents the most refined, the most extreme, version yet of Kundera's idea of the novel.

'A book which is not a copy of other books has its own construction,' warned Lawrence and the kind of novels I like are ones which bear no traces of *being* novels. Which is why the novelists I like best are, with the exception of the last-named, not novelists at all: Nietzsche, the Goncourt brothers, Barthes, Fernando Pessoa, Ryszard Kapuscinski, Thomas Bernhard...

* * *

Well, it's been a hectic couple of months. Action-packed. You won't believe what I've done.

Only bought a flat in *Oxford*. Yes, really. Unbelievable but true. Oxford! Now if there is one place on earth where you cannot, where it is physically impossible to write a book about Lawrence it is here, in Oxford. You could write a book about plenty of writers in Oxford: Hardy, or Joyce even – people are probably doing just that, even now, dozens of them – but not Lawrence. If there is one person you cannot write a book about here, in Oxford, it is Lawrence. So I have made doubly sure that there is no chance of my finishing my study of Lawrence: he is the one person you cannot write about here, in Oxford; and Oxford is the one place where you cannot write about Lawrence.

When I say you can't possibly write a book about Lawrence in Oxford that is not to be taken too literally. At this moment, within a few miles of my flat, dozens of people are probably writing books about Lawrence. That tapping I can hear through my open window is probably someone writing a book or a thesis or preparing a lecture, or, at the very least, doing an *essay* on D. H. Lawrence. It can be done. It can be done – but it can't be done, it shouldn't be done. You can't write a half-decent book about Lawrence in Oxford, can't write any kind of book about Lawrence without betraying him totally. By doing so you immediately disqualify yourself, render yourself ineligible. It is like spitting on his grave.

So why did I do it? I ask myself. Why did I do it? I had to live somewhere. You have to live somewhere. This is the awful truth, the latest increment of the immense fund of wisdom that I have been building up over the years. You have to live somewhere. Wherever you are, you have to live somewhere. And not Rome, I decided. Oh, I got into a terrible state there. The winter was cold and Rome is one of the worst places to be when it is cold. We were cold at home, cold in cafés, cold in pizzerias and cold on the buses we were forced to take because it was too cold to be on the moped. Staying in was cold, going out was colder. It was uncharacteristically cold, apparently. This is how Romans cope with the cold: every year everyone declares 'it never gets this cold' and in this way, even though it gets this cold every year, enough rhetorical heat is generated to get through the unseasonably seasonable cold. You are better off in a seriously cold place like England.

The cold got me thinking about telly. All the time that we were in Rome, listening to people say it never gets this cold, I kept thinking how happy I would be if I were back in England, watching *Grandstand*, watching Rugby League in near-blizzard conditions while I was *indoors* watching telly. That's how I endured the winter in Rome. While everyone else endured the winter by saying 'it never gets this cold' I endured it by imagining I was in England watching telly, watching Rugby League. Lawrence was right: 'One's native land has a sort of hopeless attraction, when one is away.' But it was an attraction that was easy for him and Rilke to resist:

there wasn't any telly to tempt them back. Telly, lovely telly. I began buying English papers just to see what I was missing on telly. To be precise, I began buying English papers because I began missing English papers – even though I had never actually read English papers while I was in England – and then I began scrutinising the telly pages of the English papers even though I never used to watch telly in England, even though the papers usually arrived in Rome a day late so that I ended up studying schedules of programmes that had already been broadcast. It wasn't homesickness, this longing to watch English telly. It may *sound* like homesickness, may even be one of the classic symptoms of homesickness, but it wasn't homesickness. I'd left that behind years ago and despised anyone who suffered from it. I didn't even know what it was any more. No, my telly-sickness was part of a larger anguish, a sickness in search of a home, a free-floating anxiety that could never put down roots and, as a consequence, kept shifting, changing direction and form, one moment manifesting itself as a desire to watch English telly, the next as an *overwhelming* desire to watch English telly. I'd felt the same thing before, in Paris, but had been able to assuage it by going to the cinema. In Italy, though, it is virtually impossible to go to the cinema because all films are ruined by being dubbed into Italian.

'Why don't you learn Italian?' said Laura. 'Then we could go to the cinema.'

'That is not the point,' I said. 'The point is that I have a basic respect for the medium and refuse to see it violated. Italy should not even be allowed to show films. All film distributors should boycott Italy until they stop dubbing.' Actually, on Monday nights, one or two cinemas in Rome *do* show films in the original language but they ruin them by having intermissions. An Italian can't go for more than forty minutes without having something sweet, a *cornetto* or *gelato*, and so any films which are not already ruined by being dubbed into Italian are ruined by being carved up into forty-minute portions. What children they are, Italians!

I went on and on about this to Laura, about how Italians were a race of children and she became understandably angry, not as angry as she became, though, about actual children. Having children had never been an issue between us but suddenly it was. We had discussed getting a pet a few times (to my great surprise I discovered, at the age of thirty-six, that I was a dog-lover) but children, children! Larkin thought it strange that in his letters, Lawrence, 'the least reticent of men', never once alluded to the possibility of having children. Even if that's true – and I have a feeling it's not – I find it strange that Larkin was so surprised by this. I like the way Lawrence had no children because I hate children and I hate parents of children: the fact that all anyone did in England was have children was one of the things that drove me out of that crèche of a country, that crèche of a country that I've moved back to.

The quarrel with Laura was essentially a semantic one. She wanted me to qualify my position – 'I never want to have children' – into something more moderate, something which at least kept the possibility alive. Failing that, she said, if I was so adamant about not wanting children, why didn't I have a vasectomy?

'That's an easy one,' I said. 'Because it might be painful.' But I also wondered if my absolute refusal to consider the possibility of ever having children – not just a lack of desire to have them but a vehement desire to not have them – might not be the psychological manifestation of physical sterility. I'd never made anyone pregnant which, for a man of my age, was unusual. So why not go to the hospital and have myself checked out so that we could avoid the palaver of contraception? Because I know what I'm like, I know myself too well. If it turned out that I *was* sterile then I can guarantee that within a year I would be hell-bent on adopting a Romanian orphan – either that or shelling out fortunes for some state-of the-art fertility treatment.

I was particularly unresponsive to Laura's request to moderate my position on children because this took place just after Christmas and everyone was complaining that they had had to spend the holidays with in-laws, with X's relatives, with Y's mother . . . Life for people with children is crammed with obligations and duties to be fulfilled. Nothing is done for pleasure. The child becomes a source of restrictive obligation. Even the desire to have children is expressed in terms of fulfilling a biological duty. The lies people lead!

The perfect life, the perfect lie, I realised after Christmas, is one which prevents you from doing that which you would ideally have done (painted, say, or written unpublishable poetry) but which, in fact, you have no wish to do. People need to feel that they have been thwarted by *circumstances* from pursuing the life which, had they led it, they would not have wanted; whereas the life they really want is precisely a compound of all those thwarting circumstances. It is a very elaborate, extremely simple procedure, arranging this web of self-deceit: contriving to convince yourself that you were prevented from doing what you wanted. Most people don't want what they want: people want to be prevented, restricted. The hamster not only loves his cage, he'd be lost without it. That's why children are so convenient: you have children because you're struggling to get by as an artist – which is actually what being an artist means – or failing to get on with your career. *Then* you can persuade yourself that your children prevented you from having this career that had never looked like working out. So it goes on: things are always forsaken in the name of an obligation to someone else, never as a failing, a falling short of yourself. Before you know it desire has atrophied to the degree that it can only make itself apparent by passing itself off as an obligation. After a couple of years of parenthood people become incapable of saying what they want to do in terms of what they want to do. Their preferences can only be articulated in terms of a hierarchy of obligations – even though it is by fulfilling these obligations (visiting in-laws, being forced to stay in and baby-sit) that they scale the summit of their desires. The self-evasion does not stop there: at some level they are ashamed because they realise that these desires are so paltry as barely even to merit the name of desires and so these feeble desires have to take on the guise of an obligation.

I ranted on to Laura about this night after night. I was feeling all these things particularly acutely because, at that time, I was failing to make any progress with my study of Lawrence and this failure played a crucial part in my succumbing to a deep depression which I will discuss in detail later. The long and the short of it was that I became convinced that I needed a job, a day job, something with minimal responsibilities which would impose some discipline, some routine on me, something which would stop me indulging myself all day long seven days a week. If I had a job,

I thought, I might even make more progress with my study of Lawrence because then I would value my free time. I could work in a shop, say, and all the time I was there I would be looking forward to knocking off, to going home and getting down to work on my study of Lawrence. As it was, as things stood in Rome, as they had stood in Alonissos, as they had stood for many years irrespective of where I was living, I had nothing to keep me from writing my study of Lawrence, and so I never buckled down to it. If I had a three-day-a-week job, I reasoned, I would get more done in the remaining four than I did at the moment with seven at my disposal. Such an arrangement would distance me from Lawrence who, once he had given up teaching, never considered getting a part-time job in a shop or anywhere else, but I was losing faith in what might be termed 'method' criticism and, if truth be told, I was losing interest in Lawrence. More precisely I had lost interest in my study of Lawrence. This all came to a head after our ill-fated trip to Oaxaca, which I will return to later, but the upshot of all this was that I believed that I had to get a job and since I couldn't possibly get a job in Italy – I had, needless to say, made no attempt to learn Italian – my thoughts which were already turning towards telly in England now became focused on a job in England. I began to think I would love a life in England, working at a nice part-time job and then watching telly in the evenings and, if the urge took me, doing some work on my study of Lawrence which, instead of being this daunting undertaking, would assume the status of a hobby, something I could get on with in odd moments, when there was nothing on telly.

So here I am, here we are – Laura's sister is sub-letting the apartment in Rome – in Oxford. Laura likes it. I hate it, needless to say, am sick of watching telly and have already abandoned any thought of getting part-time employment. As soon as I got back to England, back to this grim little rock, I felt myself shrinking. Back in the land where I belonged, back among my own tribe, I immediately missed *not* belonging, missed that strange home you can build out of homelessness, out of not belonging. And at the same time, coexisting easily with the feeling it apparently contradicted, was the feeling that I did not belong here, that there was no place for me here, that I was more at home in Rome where I had never felt at home for a moment.

And overlaying all of this was the sense that this hatred of England was not entirely authentic, that I felt this way because it was a Lawrentian sentiment, that what I was actually experiencing was plagiarised emotion. I was not the first person to suffer from this condition. From France, in 1961, John Osborne dispatched his infamous 'Letter to my Countrymen': 'This is a letter of hate. It is for you my countrymen. I mean those men of my country who have defiled it . . . Damn you, England. You're rotting now, and quite soon you'll disappear. My hate will outrun you yet, if only for a few seconds. I wish it could be eternal.'

Signed 'In sincere and utter hatred', it was dashed off, apparently, in response to the escalating crisis of the Cold War, but what Osborne was really excited about was the chance to sound like Lawrence. A year earlier he had accused the English of 'living in a world without wonder'; a year later his loathing for Hugh Gaitskell was validated by appeal to a Lawrentian ideal: 'the root of living'. But in the summer of 1961, in Valbonne, he was virtually *quoting* Lawrence. It was not just that Lawrence offered a template for anti-English indignation, he provided the letter of the text: 'Curse you, my countrymen, you have put the halters round your necks, and pull tighter, from day to day,' he had written. 'You are strangling yourselves, you blasted fools. Oh my countrymen . . .' That was in 1912; by 1917, after the authorities refused to endorse his passport, thereby sabotaging his plans to leave for America, Lawrence was even more vehement: 'I curse my country with my soul and body, it is a country accursed physically and spiritually. Let it be accursed forever, accursed and blasted. Let the seas swallow it, let the waters cover it, so that it is no more. And let it be known as accursed England, the country of the damned. I curse it, I curse England, I curse the English, man, woman, and child, in their nationality let them be accursed and hated and never forgiven.'

I enjoyed these sentiments, enjoyed them even more when I was expressing them myself. It was a sign of Englishness, this lambasting of England and Englishness. 'If thine eye offend thee pluck it out – but I am English and my Englishness is my very vision,' Lawrence declared, recognising this tendency in himself. 'This is my own, my native land,' I said to myself: land of rules where if anything is fun it is illegal; where, if you are sitting on a bus, it is all but impossible to conceal your loathing of the people around you but you do conceal it, somehow, because all around your fellow-passengers are somehow concealing *their* loathing of *you*. Ah yes, hating England from abroad was one thing but it didn't compare with the real thing, with hating it while you were there.

As for Oxford, or Dullford to give it its proper name, a cloud of stupidity, of extreme mental fatigue, hangs over the place because of all these dim-wit academics shovelling away at their research, digging the graves of literature. Contrary to popular belief Oxford has the highest concentration of dull-witted, stupid, narrow-minded people anywhere in the British Isles. Fact. Oh, I hate it – and for that reason it's absolutely perfect. Now that I'm here in Dullford, in England, all I want is to be back in Rome but rather than being a source of torment this brings peace of mind. Now that I have a place in England I have no desire to be here, I'm free to wander the world as before – except that before, when I didn't really live anywhere, I was overwhelmed by anxiety about where I was going to live, was desperate to be back in England.

That anguish, that uncertainty, became more and more intense as time went by but I wonder now if it was not akin to the burning that a rocket experiences as it passes through the earth's atmosphere and into space; if it was not, in my case, the friction felt before passing into some zone of total liberation: a last tug of gravity tempting me to settle. Perhaps I experienced it so strongly precisely because this resistance was making itself felt for the last time, because the last root was about to give way.

Birds in flight, claims the architect Vincenzo Volentieri, are not *between* places, they carry their places with them. We never wonder where they live: they are at home in the sky, in flight. Flight is their way of being in the world. If I could have stuck it out a little longer maybe I could have become bird-like, at home in flight, free. But who knows? Maybe that moment of total letting-go, of utter liberation, never comes. In which case maybe it was the right decision to move to Dullford – especially since now that I am here I have no desire to be here. Now that I have a place, a base, I am free to wander without the anguish of wondering where to live. It is difficult to become a bird but it is relatively easy to become a boat: if you have a harbour you can drift far away from it. So now I have a harbour, a lovely little two-bedroom nest-harbour in Dullford, conveniently located for local shops, bus and train stations, within easy reach of Heathrow . . .

That's one way of looking at it but I know I've let myself down, sold myself short. 'It is the capitulation a man has to make sooner or later,' Lawrence wrote to Edward McDonald on hearing that he had bought a house. 'The tortoise makes his hundred paces, then takes firmly to his shell.' On the brink of becoming a bird I settled for being a tortoise. Rilke was right:

> We can so easily
> slip back from what we have struggled to attain,
> abruptly, into a life we never wanted;
> can find that we are trapped, as in a dream,
> and die there, without ever waking up.

Were I to die now, in Oxford, today, it would be the most awful end to my life, everything accomplished would be belittled by this fact. And since I don't want to *die* here, what am I doing *living* in the town where I went to university, forty miles along the A40 from the town where I went to school, where I was born, where my dad was born?

'The tragedy of Lawrence the working-class boy is that he did not live to come home.' I remember, very clearly, the first time I read this, fifteen years ago, in *Culture and Society*. I was on a bus in Brixton and Raymond Williams's remark seemed one of the most pertinent and poignant things anyone had ever written about Lawrence. There it was: the last word on

Lawrence. It wasn't just that Williams was right about Lawrence: I *believed* what he said, almost as an article of faith.

Only now can I see how wrong Williams was. This might have been the tragedy of Lawrence the working-class boy but to see Lawrence in these terms, to see him as the working-class boy, is to sell him short in much the same way that Frieda considered Leavis had done ('from *The Rainbow* on,' she chided, 'Lawrence is no longer a British writer, but a universal one'). The trajectory of Lawrence's life was not to leave his origins behind but to go beyond them.

How wrong Williams is becomes obvious as early as 'The Return Journey', the final section of *Twilight in Italy*. At an inn Lawrence meets an Englishman, a clerk who is on a walking holiday. 'Holiday', as Lawrence discovers, is hardly the right word, for the young man from Streatham has set himself a gruelling itinerary to cram into his two weeks' annual leave. When Lawrence meets him he has almost accomplished his goal but is 'sick with fatigue and over-exhaustion'. At first Lawrence is aghast at his determination and courage, then shocked to discover that after this heroic exertion of willpower he is going back to London – to the machine. The fact that the Englishman's awful itinerary was effectively controlled by London, by the machine, makes Lawrence flinch: 'His eyes were dark and deep with unfathomable courage. Yet he was going back in the morning. He was going back. All he had courage for was to go back. He would go back, though he died by inches. Why not? It was killing him, it was like living loaded with irons. But he had the courage to submit, to die that way, since it was the way allotted to him.' Lawrence would later describe the men going off to fight in

France in almost identical terms; now, torn between admiration and horror, he responds with pity: 'My heart was wrung for my countryman, wrung till it bled.' This equipoise of emotion cannot be maintained for long: in the morning when Lawrence gets up to find the clerk gone there is a characteristic and convulsive change in feeling: 'Suddenly I hated him. The dogged fool, to keep his nose on the grindstone like that. What was all his courage but the very tip-top of cowardice.'

Lawrence resumes his own journey and then pauses on a hill. 'I looked down the direction of the furka, and thought of my tired Englishman from Streatham, who would be on his way home. Thank God I need not go home: never perhaps.' This, for me, is one of the huge moments in Lawrence, tossed out in passing, not dwelt upon, but looking way beyond Williams – and back to Nietzsche. Back, precisely, to *Human, All Too Human*, to the preface in which Nietzsche describes a crucial stage in the evolution of the 'free spirit'. At certain moments, writes Nietzsche, a person undertaking 'the dangerous privilege of living *experimentally*' will experience 'a pale, subtle happiness of light and sunshine, a feeling of bird-like freedom, bird-like altitude, bird-like exuberance, and a third thing in which curiosity is united with a tender contempt'. At his 'bird-like altitude' in the Alps Lawrence experiences exactly this sudden, liberating surge that renders an entire life worthwhile because it has led to this moment when you are in the middle of your destiny, ready to accept anything that comes. Given Lawrence's circumstances that day, Nietzsche's imagery could hardly be more apposite: in a book written for those 'free spirits' who do not yet exist, whose path he is hoping to ease into the world, it is as if he is *describing* Lawrence's feelings; conversely, Lawrence, at this moment, is, as it were, *reading* Nietzsche.

Oh, and *I* know that feeling; I've experienced it in New Orleans, in Algiers, even, at odd moments, in Sweden where the temperature only climbed above zero once in the six frozen weeks I spent there – but there is no chance of ever feeling it in Dullford, in England...

One of Rilke's last important poems was written in August 1926, a few months before his death. Here is part of it in Jeremy Reed's free adaptation:

> To know serenity the dove must fly
> far from its dovecote, its trajectory
> informs it, distance, fear, the racing sky
> are only understood in the return.
>
> The one that stayed at home, never tested
> the boundaries of loss, remained secure,
> only those who win back are ever free
> to contemplate a newer, surer flight.

But *when* do you return? For a long time I thought that the contentment I experienced when I did finally settle would be the more intense – if contentment can become more *intense* without becoming something less contented; perhaps contentment is precisely a *lack* of intensity – for having been postponed so long. Only to discover that there was no contentment, that there was in fact no change at all, at best there was a temporary muffling of discontent which was soon making itself felt as powerfully as before.

Rilke's poem also ignores a possibility that it cannot but suggest: that after a while one acquires a resistance to returning, that one's capacity for contentment is diminished by the flight into adventure. Perhaps the further you fly from home the more stifling home becomes. One returns not to serenity but to a sensation of suffocation which can only be alleviated by further wrenching departures. Seen in this light, Lawrence became a prisoner of departures, his capacity for contentment diminished by constant travelling. Hence the increasingly desperate tone in which he ended up asking various friends *where* he might live.

Bear in mind also that although Rilke's poem ends with the idea of return, its emotional trajectory inexorably suggests a realm of contentment which can be enjoyed only by those who abandon any idea of returning, who keep going, who make their home in flight. If the dove that 'ventures outside' returns to 'know serenity', what does the bird experience who keeps going? This leads to the imperative, beyond Rilke, suggested by that admonition of Neruda's: 'He who returns has never left.' Lawrence had a premonition of this idea at the Gotthard Pass and at moments he surrendered to it as if to a destiny. 'I feel I shall wander for the rest of my days. But I don't care.'

There is a moment in Ian McEwan's novel *The Child in Time* when, asked by his young son why the railway lines 'grew together as they got further away', the father 'squinted into the distance where question and answer converged'. In a similar, light-hearted way Lawrence saw that there was a point where Rilke and Neruda converged: 'Oh Schwiegermutter it must be so,' he wrote from Australia, 'it is my destiny, to wander. But the world is round, brings us again back to Baden.'

He is an extremely complex case, Lawrence. Traces of all the potentialities and ambiguities of Rilke's poem can be found in his life. What is certain, though, is that his restlessness, his desire to move on stayed with him to the last. 'This place no good': these were the final words of what, in many editions, is printed as his last letter. He was referring to the sanatorium, where he died, the aptly-named 'Ad Astra'. What better corrective to the concealed assumption within Rilke's poem – to the commonly held belief – that there will at some point *be* some serenity, some contentment?

The essence of Lawrence's life and writing is away from the notion of achieving some permanent state of unruffled serenity. Never content simply to record his transitory feelings and surges of emotion, Lawrence was always wanting to turn them into some permanent testimony, into a 'philosophy' – and no writer was temperamentally less suited to do so. Lawrence is at his best when he is recording his fleeting moods and impressions without trying to fit them into any kind of design, even the artistic one of a novel. The endless fascination of the letters lies in his bottomless capacity for change – from blazing anger to good humour in the space of a few hours or minutes – his capacity to recover from any setback, to always give life, to always give himself, one more chance.

Films and books urge us to think that there will come certain moments in our lives when, if we can make some grand, once-in-a-lifetime gesture of relinquishment, or of standing up for a certain principle – if we can throw in our job and head off, leave the safe life with a woman that we do not love and, as it were, *come out* – then we will be liberated, free. Moments – crises – like these are crucial to the cinema or theatre where psychological turmoil has to be externalised and compressed. Dramatically speaking what happens after moments such as these is unimportant even though the drama continues afterwards, with the consequences of these sudden lurches beyond the quotidian. Up until then the question is what you are freeing yourself *from*; the real question, however, as Nietzsche points out – and Lawrence repeats in his Nietzschean *Study of Thomas Hardy* – is free *for* what?

Unless, like Thelma and Louise, you plunge off the side of a canyon, there is no escaping the everyday. What Lawrence's life demonstrates so powerfully is that it actually takes a daily effort to be free. To be free is not the result of a moment's decisive action but a project to be constantly renewed. More than anything else, freedom requires tenaciousness. There are intervals of repose but there will never come a state of definitive rest where you can give up because you have turned freedom into a permanent condition. Freedom is always precarious. That is what Rilke, who dogs these pages like a shadow, meant when he wrote of falling back into a life we never wanted. Lawrence warned John Middleton Murry of the same thing: 'Either you go on wheeling a wheelbarrow and lecturing at Cambridge and going softer and softer inside, or you make a hard fight with yourself, pull yourself up, harden yourself, throw your feelings down the drain and face the world as a fighter. – You won't though.' And now I won't either.

'Freedom is a gift inside one's soul,' Lawrence declared. 'You can't have it if it isn't in you.' A gift it may be but it is not there for the taking. To realise this capacity in yourself is a struggle. Of what, then, did Lawrence's hard-won freedom consist?

Catherine Carswell applauded Lawrence for the way 'he did nothing that he did not really want to do, and all that he most wanted to do he did'. Accused, in his poem 'The Life with a Hole', of living up to the second half of Carswell's claim – *'you've always done what you want'* – Larkin grumbles that he has succeeded only in living down to the first: 'what the old ratbags mean/ Is I've never done what I don't'. For his part, Lawrence felt there had to be more to freedom than doing what one wanted – but how could one be free if one could *not* do as one wanted? He gnawed away at this constantly, resolving it by elevating the idea of what one wanted not just to a determining principle but to an obligation to one's self. 'Elevating' is perhaps not the right word for this meant fathoming one's *deepest* desires – and remaining faithful to them.

One of Lawrence's most eloquent declarations of personal liberty is expressed in terms of a vehemently indifferent retort: 'My wife and I have lived on 37 dollars a month before now: and always with sang froid. I doubt if I make more than 400 per annum now – and knock about Europe as I like, and spit in the face of anybody who tries to insult me.' To take on the world like this is also to test oneself: that, for Lawrence, is the *challenge of freedom*.

'The only history is a mere question of one's struggle inside oneself,' he declared, and in the midst of this struggle a man gained a sense of his 'his inner destiny'. In practice this meant a great deal of chopping and changing, deciding and undeciding – so much so that Lawrence's own surges and reversals of intent sometimes left him mystified. 'We had almost booked our passage to America, when suddenly it came over me I must go to Ceylon.' On occasions doing what one wants actually means pursuing a course that, superficially, one has no wish to. By assenting to these decisions of his as if to an impersonal authority Lawrence gradually and tentatively began to have a sense of a destiny that could be followed only by being forged. The perpetual questions of where to go next, whether to stay or move on, become crucial stations in the itinerary of one's destiny. In this light Lawrence's wandering becomes purposeful, and the gap between resignation and active creation almost insignificant. 'It is my destiny, to wander,' he claimed on several occasions, resigning himself to the life he had actively created: 'Really, why does one write! Or why does one write the things I write? I suppose it's destiny, but on the whole, an unkind one.'

A destiny is not something that awaits us, it is something we have to achieve in the midst of innumerable circumstantial impediments and detours. A character in *A Question of Geography* by John Berger and Nella Bielski expresses this concisely:

> Each one of us comes into the world with her or his unique possibility – which is like an aim, or, if you wish, almost like a law. The job of our lives is to become – day by day, year by year, more conscious of that aim so that it can at last be realised.

I would quibble with that 'at last': a destiny is not what is finally achieved but the act of incrementally nudging towards it. This reservation aside, Berger and Bielski express a manifesto of destiny. Precisely because of its manifold uncertainties and contradictions, Lawrence's life shows what this involves on the most practical level imaginable: which buses to take, to where, for how long . . .

'Basically it's none of our business how somebody manages to grow,' wrote Rilke, 'if only he does grow, if only we're on the trail of our own growth.' But it is quite possible that what one imagines to be the trail of one's growth is actually the path of one's diminution. It can be your destiny, in other words, not to live up to your destiny, to fall short of it, to end up in Dullford.

Needless to say I made no progress with my study of Lawrence after moving to Dullford: I was too busy DIYing. I went at it with a vengeance, painting so furiously that I even had a Kafkaesque dream: that my hands had been transformed into a pair of giant rollers.

I say I made no progress but, in the same way that Rilke wondered if our most idle days might not be our most productive, I wonder if these days spent DIYing might not have been crucial to my work on Lawrence. Lawrence as DIYer might yet turn out to be a major theme of this study. When my agent wrote to see if I was making any progress I simply copied out, by way of reply, a letter Lawrence sent to his publisher. 'Naturally I don't write when I slave building the house – my arms feel so heavy, like a navvy's, though they look as thin as ever.' My sentiments, my arms, exactly. The difference is that Lawrence was a great DIYer, perhaps the first great DIYer in English literature. 'I have painted windowframes by the mile, doors by the acre, painted a chest of drawers till it turned into a bureau, and am not through by a long chalk.' And not just painting. 'Lawrence was always busy,' Frieda's third husband, Angelo Ravagli, remembered, 'mostly doing housework.' When he was not building sheds and cupboards, putting up shelves and repairing outhouses he was doing 'the washing, cooking, floor-cleaning and everything': *making home*, in short. Once again I am struck by unexpected felicity, by how appropriate it was that I should have been drawn to Ikea on my way to Eastwood: a prime example, it now seems, of the detour as straight line. Lawrence the prophet of sexual revolution means almost nothing to us, to me, today; what I love is Lawrence the handyman. The perfect photo of Lawrence, the one that best expresses what he means to us now, on the brink of the millennium, would be one showing him hammer in hand, building an Ikea kitchen at the ranch in New Mexico.

If only *I* liked doing things like that. I love the idea of home improvement but the reality of it is that I am hopeless at it, hate it in fact. The truth is that I have now *been* to Ikea. Laura and I drove to the one in west London and had an hour of intensive therapy with a kitchen-planning consultant who persuaded us that if we read the instructions carefully and were patient then we could build our own kitchen. Laura was dubious, I was eager, and so we lugged back our selection of flat-packs and got stuck into it the very next day. Two days later we had partially (mis)assembled one unit and our dream kitchen lay stacked up in the living room awaiting the arrival of professional fitters. It was an absurdly ambitious project and so we went for something easier: putting up a cork notice-board. All my life I had dreamed of owning a cork notice-board. For years, having a cork notice-board on which one pinned bills, postcards and concert tickets was the very symbol of a settled life. And when we moved to

Dullford I bought one! Putting it up promised to be a simple business except nothing is simple in DIY: the drill went haywire and gouged a crater in the plaster. Already angry I moved a couple of inches to the left and made a neat hole that plunged – BANG! – straight into the electric cable. Complete blackout. Plus I had a terrible shock, namely that I didn't get any kind of *electric* shock (some kind of insulation in the drill, I suppose) and, in this disoriented state of shocked unshockedness, took a screwdriver to the noticeboard and slashed it to ribbons.

I blame my father. DIYing is all about measuring, checking and re-checking; it's about patience and precision, and I have none because my father emphasised all these things to me at such an early age that he took all the fun out of DIYing. To put the fun back into it I go at it hammer and tongs and the results are disastrous and not much fun. And *still* I love the idea of it, love those cathedrals of our self-help era, the home improvement superstores, I mean, especially Do It All where the PR booms out updates on special discounts, each bulletin ending with the assurance that 'Together We Can Do It All'. And it works, this home-owners' call to prayer. You hear and you believe. You have faith. Only when you get back to the home you want to improve do you find that, alone, you can do nothing.

Together, though, together with my father, it was possible to put up two hundred feet of bookshelves in my study. I measured the room, drew up the plans and, together, my father and I bought, transported and varnished the wood which was transformed into two hundred feet of shelving. My father did most of the measuring, a lot of the sawing and all the drilling. He made some mistakes in the measuring or the spirit-levelling and consequently some of the shelves were about an inch out of horizontal. He couldn't account for it and I could see how it hurt and mystified him, that discrepancy. There was no explaining it, except to say he was losing it, losing his eye, his accuracy. To compensate he built some special wooden wedges so that the shelves ended up inch-perfect.

I'm looking at them now, those shelves which will probably turn out to be my father's last great piece of DIY. At some time in the future – the hypothetical future, the one that will never come to pass because I hope to God I never have a child – my son will expect me to put up shelves for him. It is a biological law: the father builds shelves for his children. What I wonder, though, is where this ability to put up shelves is going to come from. When I was young I was always struck by the large manliness of my father's hands. When, I asked myself, would my hands become like his? For the poet Michael Hofmann it started to happen in his late twenties:

> By now, it is almost my father's arm,
> a man's arm, that lifts the cigarettes to my mouth . . .

Hofmann's father was a writer so it is not surprising that the arm of his poet son should have turned out the same way. But for me, I think, it is never going to happen. My father's hands and all the skills – drilling, sawing, building – that culminated in them have been left behind. From now on my hands will write the cheques that pay the kitchen-fitters, men with hands like my father's, to build the things that he – like Lawrence – could make for himself and his son. It is not just a class you leave, it's your biology too. Or maybe that's not quite true.

'The photograph of father came today. It's very nice: I see a good deal of myself in it.' That was in January 1925, four months after Lawrence's father had died. A few days ago my mother gave me a photograph of my father when he was in his mid-twenties. He is dressed in tennis whites, a blazer draped over his shoulders, racket in one hand. Only the blurred council house in the background – where his sister, my auntie Joan, still lives – insists that this is not an image from the long afternoon of the English leisured class. His hair – already thinning – is slicked back. Give or take a few years and details of fashion he looks as I do now: the same long legs, the same thin wrists, the same eyes and mouth. For the first time, I see myself in a picture of my father.

A few weeks earlier, to use up the last frames of her film, Laura took some pictures of me after I had finished playing tennis. My back was aching, I was dehydrated – we had drunk too much red wine the night before – but I was surprised, when the pictures came back from the lab, by just how terrible I looked. Something of that weariness made me look like my father as he does now, in his seventies. For the first time I saw my father in a picture of myself.

The reciprocal relation of these photos – mirror-images, reflecting each other back across a generational divide of almost forty years – is not accidental. It is a visual preparation for my father's inevitable death: there will come a time when it is only my genes that will continue the work of the camera in preserving his likeness. Looking at that picture of my father in his tennis whites, I realised how that skill, that instinctive ability to hit a ball in motion, to get the hang of sports, is still there, in my hands, in my arms.

They gave me pause, those photos, made me wonder what other traits I had inherited. One night I was woken by the sound of the people next door getting back late, by the key scraping in their lock. Lying in bed, suddenly awake, I realised that another part of my character could now be firmly identified as a permanent trait. I have always woken up easily but it is only now that I can collate the evidence of the years into the simple verdict: I am a light sleeper. Like my father. When I lived at home the slightest noise was always enough to rouse him. Light sleeping, for him, was always a kind of domestic vigilance, a way of being alert to any possible intrusion into his home and family: a way of looking after my mother and me. A light sleeper himself, he took great pains to avoid waking the rest of us when he got up in the semi-darkness to go to work; like him I open doors quietly and walk lightly across rooms.

These habits were acquired as if by accident; others, like paying debts promptly, scrupulously, were conscientiously instilled. It may be of no interest to anyone – and this entire book, I suspect, is of no interest to anyone – but it so happens that I am very good at paying my debts. You can tell, just by looking at me. I have an honest face, apparently. Grocers never refuse when I ask if I can owe them for milk or vegetables and quite often they tell me it is because I have an honest face. It is one of the things grocers pride themselves on, judging character by appearance. If they have the knack for picking out the best vegetables at markets then they can pick out customers who can owe them money for their under-ripe melons and rotten apples. Shopkeepers were happy to extend Lawrence credit, I imagine, since he was always scrupulous about paying his debts. Maybe this shared quality is why I like reading what are ostensibly his dullest letters, the ones in which he settles accounts, reckons up what he owes. 'I owe you some money,' he wrote to Bertrand Russell. 'We got those frescoes for 3 guineas. That is, your share, 31/6. Therefore I owe you 8/6. I will send it you, I won't forget.' I love that 'I won't forget', and I love it when he urged Barbara Low to 'remind Frieda that she pays you for the cake etc. I shall be *so* angry with her if she forgets it, as she is too likely to'. Three weeks later he wrote again: 'Of course Frieda never paid you for the cake and sweets so I send on here the 10/-.'

The corollary of this scrupulousness was, needless to say, a tendency towards niggardliness. He complains that his sister Emily 'can't help feeling that ninepence is exactly half as good again as sixpence. If I wearily protest that ninepence is nothing to me unless it's ninepence worth of life, she just looks at me as if I'd said nothing. How I *hate* the attitude of ordinary people to life. How I loathe ordinariness! How from my soul I abhor nice simple people, with eternal price lists.' That's as may be but she can hardly have been more obsessed with prices than her brother. Some of his best letters are nothing *but* price lists. Others are long, itemised whinges about how much things are costing, how he is being overcharged, how the exchange rate is working to his disadvantage (especially in Italy), how he has to pay duty on books sent through the post, how he is being cheated by government officials, shopkeepers, hoteliers and porters. As a travel book *Sea and Sardinia* is way ahead of its time: it anticipates the era of mass tourism when the chief conviction of all English holiday-makers is that they are being fleeced at every turn, when the strongest memory of the Sistine Chapel will be the stunning price of the choc-ices on sale outside. Lawrence is in a strop about money for the duration of his Sardinia trip but at one point his irritation erupts in molten anger.

I am thoroughly sick to death of the sound of liras. No man can overhear ten words of Italian today without two thousand or two million or ten or twenty or two liras flying like venomous mosquitoes round his ears. Liras – liras – liras – nothing else. Romantic, poetic, cypress-and-orange-tree Italy is gone. Remains an Italy smothered in the filthy smother of innumerable lira notes: ragged, unsavoury paper money so thick upon the air that one breathes it in like some greasy fog. Behind this greasy fog some people may still see the Italian sun. I find it hard work.

He found it hard work, too, to keep in temper with the various publishers and agents he felt were not treating him honestly ('Does the return railway fare from New York cost as much as $300?' he queried Robert Mountsier. 'You remember you said you would let me pay the railway fare only'). Again and again Lawrence insists that what he wants is to be frank, fair and 'precise' in his dealings. 'I don't want anything that doesn't seem to you just and fair,' he wrote to Martin Secker at the start of their business relationship. 'But I want you also to treat me justly and fairly' – something which Lawrence felt happened all too rarely.

Perhaps we should not make too much of Lawrence and money. He was, after all, a genuinely freelance writer in that he lived entirely by his pen (and the odd loan) and freelance writers are notoriously obsessed with money. I am, at any rate. When Flaubert – who, unlike Lawrence (and me), had a modest private income to live off – declared 'everybody is hard up, starting with me!' he was not only lamenting his lot, he was also striking the authentic note of literary single-mindedness. Read most writers' letters and book-writing appears to take a subordinate place to book-keeping. Because at various times he tried to do without an agent and opted, eventually, for self-publishing, it is not surprising that an exceptional amount of the seven volumes of letters comprises Lawrence's financial wrangles. What is surprising is to find that the parts of the correspondence of a great writer I most like are those which would be edited out if any kind of selection were made, i.e. those having nothing to do with his genius and everything to do with his ordinariness, with the ordinariness he claimed to loathe. The fact that Lawrence wrote *Lady Chatterley's Lover* means next to nothing to me; what matters is that he paid his way, settled his debts, made nice jam and marmalade, and put up shelves.

All of this is irrelevant – if something can be deemed irrelevant in a book comprised entirely of irrelevancies – except insofar as it confirms something about Lawrence which other people have commented on but which I now see as being literally central to him: he was always in the midst of what he was doing, was able, as Huxley noticed, 'to absorb himself completely in what he was doing at the moment'. By all accounts, he was incapable of not giving himself wholly to what he was doing: couldn't read someone else's manuscript without scribbling all over it or rewriting it, couldn't clean a floor without making it perfectly clean, couldn't do a painting without becoming a painter.

Writers always envy artists, would trade places with them in a moment if they could. The painter's life seems less ascetic, less monkish, less hunched. Instead of the austere mess of the desk there is the chaos of the studio: dirty coffee cups, paint-smudged cassette decks, drawings of the artist's girlfriend, naked, on the walls. It starts at school, this association of writing with work and art with fun: the classroom is a site of boredom and order, the art room a place to play, to mess around, to make a mess; Double Physics was the low point in the school timetable but Double Art – more even than Games which often involved exposure to harsh weather conditions and the possibility of physical injury – signalled an hour and a half of not having to work. For the writer, work is characterised by the absolute cessation of physical movement (all movement is an evasion of and distraction from the job in hand), by a suspension of life. For the painter work means a more intense physical engagement in life, it begins with carpentry (making stretchers) and ends in glazing, varnishing and framing. Even though it thereby involves *labour* the painter's work – or so it seems to the writer – never seems like work. In the age of the computer the writer's office or study will increasingly resemble the customer service desk of an ailing small business. The artist's studio, though, is still what it has always been: an erotic space. For the writer the artist's studio is, essentially, a place where women undress. Van Gogh may have warned that 'painting and fucking a lot don't go together' but the smell of white spirits and paint is suggestive of nothing else so much as afternoon sex. Personally, I would love to have been a painter.

One of the reasons that writers – rather than art critics – have written so well about artists and painting is that they retain these delusions (for such, artists assure me, they are) about picture-making. When writers write about painting they are in a sense on vicarious holiday. Lawrence, of course, went further. He not only produced some of the best writing on art in English – the 'Introduction to his Paintings' is a small, mad masterpiece – he also became a painter.

In the last years of his life painting was a greater source of fulfilment, on a day-to-day basis, than writing. What does it matter whether they are any good, these paintings? It never occurred to Lawrence to wonder whether he could paint or not. When, in the 'Introduction to his Paintings', he implicitly argued that the tradition of painting culminated in his own work, he was also arguing that an ability to paint was not the most important part of being a painter. Lawrence took his painting seriously, pursued it strenuously, but it always retained something of its idyllic character: 'Painting is a much more amusing art than writing, and much less to it, costs one less, amuses one more.' Painting was the absolute fulfilment of his ideals of work: to work to become more himself. In the same way that the photograph of Lawrence sitting by the tree – and not writing – was the idyllic image of the writer then the crowning achievement of his career as a writer was that he became a painter.

According to Huxley, Lawrence possessed 'an even more remarkable accomplishment' than an ability to paint: 'He knew how to do nothing. He could just sit and be perfectly content.'

Not like me. I am always on the edge of what I am doing. I do everything badly, sloppily, to get it over with so that I can get on to the next thing that I will do badly and sloppily so that I can then do nothing – which I do anxiously, distractedly, wondering all the time if there isn't something else I should be getting on with. 'Being with you is like licking sugar through a glass,' Laura once said. 'You're never quite there.' When I'm working I'm wishing I was doing nothing and when I'm doing nothing I'm wondering if I should be working. I hurry through what I've got to do and then, when I've got nothing to do, I keep glancing at the clock, wishing it was time to go out. Then, when I'm out, I'm wondering how long it will be before I'm back home.

The moment I finish this study, all books by and about Lawrence will be returned to the shelves that my father and I built. It's a pleasing prospect. If there's one thing that keeps me banging away at this study, in fact, it is the knowledge that one day I will be able to put all those books back on the shelf between Larkin and Lessing and, later, hopefully, will be able to put this one up there too. Essentially, I want things *over with*: I wanted to get the shelf-building over with so that I could get back to writing my book about Lawrence; now I want to get writing my book over with so that I can put it up on the shelves – and start another one.

What's more I've got no intention of changing. This is my idea of contentment.

You see I've decided to butch it out, to go in the opposite direction to that suggested by yoga and meditation. The yoga-meditation-zen path leads to peace with the world and oneness with the infinite. Petty annoyances fade into insignificance, the ego dissolves, and you are left in a state of unruffled serenity and calm. Or so I gather. It's never worked for me. Faced with the thousands of petty annoyances and grievances encountered in the course of a week I've often tried to respond with a shrugged 'Who cares?' I've said it over and over to myself like a mantra, 'Who cares? Who cares?' until I was practically screaming 'Who cares? Who cares?' Before you know it you are reproaching the world for not caring, shaking your fist at the heavens, demanding to know *why* no one cares.

That's what I'm doing: shaking my fist at the world. I won't let even the smallest grievance escape me. I'm going to seize on the most insignificant inconvenience, annoyance, hindrance, set-back, disappointment and am going to focus all my rage, anger, bitterness and frustration on it. 'I shall turn my head away,' wrote Nietzsche. 'Henceforth that will be my sole negation.' Not me. I'm going to glare right back at it. It? Anything that gets my goat or pisses me off. Nothing will escape me.

Travelling by coach, for example, the zen thing to do, obviously, is to relax into passenger-limbo, empty your head of all worries about traffic hold-ups and road-works and accept your fate. Not me. I monitor each second of the journey, looking out for seconds saved and lost. I sit at the front so that I can see the road ahead, monitor the speedometer and check that the driver is pushing the bus as hard as he can, so that I can check out traffic lights and sigh with relief when the driver gambles on the amber, or silently curse him when he is too cautiously obedient. If a passenger gets on and fumbles through his wallet for the right change, finds none and then pays by cheque I don't even attempt to read my book and think of something else: I glare and rage and inwardly curse, I mutter beneath my breath and imagine myself getting up, bawling him out and throwing him off the bus. If I'm stuck in traffic I mutter and curse beneath my breath. If I am kept waiting at a shop or supermarket I curse and mutter beneath my breath. Whatever happens I curse and mutter beneath my breath. When I am not reacting to some immediate cause of anger I am rehearsing what I am going to say to X or Y the next time I see them, thinking how I'm really going to give them an earful so that beneath my breath there is a constant rumble of abuse. You fucking stupid twat, you slow-witted mother-fucking asshole, you fucking piece of shit . . . That's it, that's what's going on in my head. Laura has said that it is obvious I am a writer because as I walk along my lips move, as if I'm talking or thinking to myself, as if I'm inventing dialogue for a book or am mentally going over some passage I've written. Yes, that's it exactly, I say, except this particular book consists entirely of variations on 'you fucking stupid cunt, I'm going to smash your fucking head in if you don't hurry up'. If anything goes wrong, anything at all, then I over-react terribly – in my head. On the surface I may grin and bear it but in my head I am thinking of wreaking a hideous vengeance on whoever it is that *seems* responsible for whatever small inconvenience I have suffered. A few days ago the local delicatessen had run out of the luxury doughnuts which I have for my elevenses and on which I depend utterly, just as I depend on my *cornetti integrali* from the Farnese when I am in Rome. Right, I thought to myself, turning on my heel and walking out, grim-faced and tight-lipped, I will return later in the day and burn the place to the ground with all the staff in it – friendly, charming staff, incidentally, who have often let me owe them money – so that they could experience a fraction of the pain that I had suffered by not being able to have my morning doughnut. It's the same at the Caffè Farnese when I am in Rome. I never *do* these terrible things and so they are kept chained up in my head, causing untold wear and tear. All the damage I dream of inflicting on the various pastry-related premises where I have experienced disappointment is actually inflicting terrible damage on my head. Sometimes I think of explaining my situation to the staff at the Farnese or at my local delicatessen. 'What you have to understand,' I imagine myself saying, 'is that I am allergic to disappointment. I have had so much disappointment in my life that the tiniest amount of it is now enough to drive me to despair. I am so brimful of disappointment that even one more tiny drop will send me spilling over the edge.' But I *don't* say that, of course, any more than I *do* go back and burn down the delicatessen or the Farnese. I keep all this rage in my head.

Who knows, though: I may hate disappointment but perhaps I also long for it. Perhaps it is not luxury doughnuts and *cornetti integrali* I want but the experience of being denied these things I think I want. Would I be so determined to have my luxury doughnut or my *cornetto integrale* every day if I knew there would always be a surplus of luxury doughnuts and *cornetti integrali*? Or have I made up my mind that I must have one of these luxury doughnuts (exceptional value, incidentally, at 35p) or *cornetti integrali* each day precisely because there is a good chance that they will not be available? Perhaps what I want, in other words, is actually not a luxury doughnut or a *cornetto integrale* but the chance to consummate my disappointment, to experience what I most dread which is actually not going doughnut- and *cornetto*-less through the day but which is, precisely, experiencing disappointment. Who knows? How can one know these things? All I do know is that for whatever reason I must have a doughnut or a *cornetto integrale* for elevenses and very frequently there are no doughnuts or *cornetti integrali* left and at those moments I would gladly take my head and dash my brains out on the shop window just to gain a brief respite from the pain that is exploding within it.

The idea behind this obsessive monitoring of all the things that enrage me is that eventually I'll become punch-drunk with annoyance. At the moment I'm in a state of exasperated exasperation, self-generating irritation, ever-increasing anger. Things annoy me now which I wouldn't even be aware of were it not for the fact that I've decided to keep a tab of things so strictly. I'm currently in a hyper-volatile condition but at some point there must come an exhaustion which is very like peace. I'll wear myself out, be so depleted by anger that I won't even have the energy to get agitated. My rage will blow itself out and I'll never raise my voice again. I'll be serene as a windless afternoon – and I got this idea, sort of, from Lawrence.

Jam-making, book-keeping and debt-paying aside, you see, what I like most about Lawrence is his temper. Not the famous, record-breaking rucks with Frieda but his day-to-day capacity for annoyance, his inexhaustible irritability. His masterpiece in this respect is a letter to Earl Brewster of 1921. 'No, I don't understand a bit what you mean about rightness and about relationships and about the world,' he begins. 'Damn the world, anyhow. And I hate "understanding" people, and I hate more still to be understood. Damn understanding more than anything. I refuse to understand you. Therefore you can say what you like, without a qualm, and never bother to alter it. I shan't understand.'

From this mild beginning Lawrence proceeds to work himself up into a fury about anything and everything. He has, we learn, 'been in a hell of a temper for three weeks'. In that time he has 'written such very spiteful letters to everybody that now the postman never comes'. It is as if the contents of the letter were so spiteful that the postman himself took offence. Now even Larkin didn't get that grouchy! And Van Gogh, he had the postman to keep him company at Arles!

At one point in the letter Lawrence's anger reaches such a pitch of fury that he abandons language and spits ink at his long-suffering friend: 'Pfui! – pish, pshaw, prrr!' After that, in more conciliatory spirit he asks Brewster: 'So, what's it like in Ceylon?' A rhetorical question if ever there was one, for as far as Lawrence is concerned he 'would rather go to Mars or the Moon. But Ceylon if there's nothing better. Is everybody there as beshitten there as here? I'll bet they are. There isn't any news, so don't ask for any.'

Lawrence was in Taormina at the time, a place he liked a great deal, more than almost any other – but one of Lawrence's enduring pleasures was to rant on about the awfulness of wherever he happened to be. Perhaps this is why Italy held such a special place in his affections: it provided constant fuel for his temper: 'I feel my summer travels didn't do much more than put me in a perfect fury with everything.

But then that's the effect most things have on me. The older I get, the angrier I become, generally. And Italy is a country to keep you in a temper from day to day: the people, I mean.'

This is from another of the bad-tempered letters he had mentioned to Brewster. Four months later, after much prevaricating about going to America he reneged on his earlier preference for the moon or Mars and went to meet the Brewsters in Ceylon. It was a place with: 'marvellous air, marvellous sun and sky – strange, vast empty country – hoary unending "bush" with a pre-primeval ghost in it – apples ripe and good, also pears . . . but – But – BUT – Well, it's always an anti-climax of buts. – I just don't want to stay, that's all . . . But I love trying things and discovering how I hate them.'

Dispatched a decade earlier, another letter expresses this familiar mood of self-generating exasperation. 'If all goes well I shall probably stay here till the spring, although neither the house nor the climate really agrees with me: this perpetual alternation between bora and sirocco is no good for the nerves, and I exhaust myself by enduring first one and then the other.'

The place in question was the Castle Duino and the author of this authentically Lawrentian moan was Rainer Maria Rilke. Rilke stayed in many of the same places as Lawrence and the overlaps of itinerary and tone alert us to the way that Lawrence's letters – and Larkin's too, perhaps – place him in the European tradition of the literature of neurasthenia, of anxiety, fretting, complaint. This tradition – more accurately, this *strain* – culminates in Thomas Bernhard, the Austrian writer who dedicated book after book to an exhaustive and exhausting catalogue of what Lawrence, writing (appropriately enough) from Austria, termed, 'the life-exhaustion feeling'. This life-exhaustion feeling in Lawrence is actually very close to that life-affirming quality that he is usually admired for. Likewise, he may have inveighed against America for the way that there was 'no life of the blood', only 'nerves, nerve-vibration, nerve-irritation' but Lawrence's famous faith in the religion of the blood often seems a disposition of the nerves.

The resemblance between Lawrence's nerve-irritation, as revealed in his letters and Bernhard's fictional neurasthenic rambling, is as striking as it is, at first, surprising. Lawrence shares with Bernhard's narrators the same chronic prevarication ('Suddenly that I am on the point of coming to America I feel I *can't* come'), intermittently, at least, the same wild misanthropy, the same loathing of their country and countrymen. Both writers display the same abrupt surges and reversals of intent, the perpetual rages that accentuate the ill health – another shared theme – by which they are, in part, generated. Both suffered badly with their lungs and in both there is the same frayed-nerve, end-of the tether quality. Some of the classic Bernhard riffs – berating the world for exactly the characteristics he is displaying in the course of his tirades, for example – are prefigured in Lawrence who declared in 1929 that he hated 'people who rave with unreasonable antipathies'. My favourite example is when he denounces Robert Mountsier as 'one of those irritating people who have generalised detestations'. *One of those* . . .

Many of the places in Lawrence's Sardinia sound uncannily like those towns in Austria that elicit Bernhard's ire. Mandas, for example, a place where, according to some people Lawrence meets, 'one does *nothing*. At Mandas one goes to bed when it's dark, like a chicken. At Mandas one walks down the road like a pig that is going nowhere. At Mandas a goat understands more than the inhabitants understand. At Mandas . . .' At Mandas even the inn is authentically Bernhardian:

> We sat at the cold table, and the lamp immediately began to wane. The room – in fact the whole of Sardinia – was stone cold, stone, stone cold. Outside the earth was freezing. Inside there was no thought of any sort of warmth: dungeon stone floors, dungeon stone walls and a dead, corpse-like atmosphere, too heavy and icy to move.

This unexpected affinity between Lawrence and Bernhard – one preoccupied by the hope, as Frieda's iconic version has it, 'of more and more life', the other with suicide and death – illuminates another characteristic that the writers share: they are both very funny. It seems ludicrous to say so but I value Lawrence increasingly if not as a comic *writer* then certainly as a comic *figure* – never more so than when he is in one of his tempers – which is most of the time. In Taos, after one of the quarrels that regularly erupted there, Tony Luhan stormed off, leaving his wife Mabel to seek comfort from Frieda. 'So Mabel thought that *she* had an angry husband?' writes a recent biographer. 'Lawrence was angry even in his sleep, Frieda declared, and proved it by taking Mabel in to witness the spectacle of Lawrence mumbling and groaning in his sleep.' Now this is the Lawrence I love. Frieda too, I suspect.

Claudio Magris identifies a recurring figure in European literature as the man who records all the little inconveniences life inflicts upon him and, in so doing, triumphs over them. Lawrence keeps saying he doesn't care about publishers, about money, about Middleton Murry and all the other 'canaille' out there in the world but when we compile a list of all the things he doesn't care about it amounts to a great anthology of grievance and complaint. Then there are the little inconveniences which resist simple solution – things being broken or mislaid or needing to be replaced – and which turn the letters into a vast saga of irritation.

Take the episode of the typewriter ribbon. On 4 July 1916, when he was finishing off *Women in Love*, Lawrence wrote to Kot asking him to get 'a black ribbon for a Smith Premier No 2 typewriter'. Kot dutifully obliged but three days later Lawrence is writing to him to say that the ribbon 'is just twice *too wide* for my machine, which takes a ribbon not more than half an inch wide. I have never seen a ribbon so wide as this. Ought I to double it, fold it? – or must I send it back and have it changed?' On 10 July he did exactly that and on the 17th the long-suffering Kot duly sent a new one which turned out to be:

> exactly like the last. I can't possibly put it on my machine. And as it arrived without a word to say who sent it, or anything like that, I am at a loss.
>
> My machine is Lawrence. C. Smith and Bros. Number 2. Perhaps I am wrong in calling it a Smith Premier. It takes a ribbon exactly half an inch wide. What then am I to do with a ribbon one-inch wide? All I want is an ordinary half-inch black ribbon. Can you solve the mystery for me?

One hardly need imagine what scenes must have erupted at the cottage in Zennor as Lawrence tried to cope with these successive ribbons. By the third week of July he was writing to Pinker saying that he had given up typing his novel ('it got on my nerves and knocked me up' and was proceeding with pencil. To Catherine Carswell he wrote even more adamantly: 'Never will I type again. It is that which has made me ill.' Not the typing *per se*, one imagines, but the exhaustion following from the rages that must have been incurred by the innumerable frustrations of trying to get the ribbon working. Then, on 1 August, it comes to an end. 'Many thanks for the ribbon,' he writes to Kot. 'This is perfect. I suppose all the mistakes came from saying "Smith Premier". I am very sorry.'

Now, nothing I have read about – or even *in* – *Women in Love* affords me as much pleasure as these letters about the Smith Premier. I read other letters in the same spirit, obsessively, eager to see what will set him off next.

One of the reasons Lawrence directed his grouchiest letter ever – *the* grouchiest letter ever? – at Brewster is because Earl and his wife Achsah were in Ceylon studying Buddhism. Lawrence had a fundamental antipathy to the peace they were searching for and which they wished on him. 'But always remember I prefer my strife,' he chided them, 'infinitely, to other people's peace, haven, and heavens.' That, I think, is a daring, beautiful preference. Comforting, too: it offers the kind of solace that Lawrence would have gleaned in 1910 when he first read Nietzsche. He expanded on this claim early in 1922, in a series of letters to Brewster which show no trace of the temper of two months previously. 'More and more I feel that meditation and the inner life are not my aim, but some sort of action and strenuousness and pain and frustration and struggling through . . . men have to fight a way for the new incarnation. And the fight and the sorrow and the loss of blood, and even the influenzas and the headaches are part of the fight and the fulfilment. Let nobody try to filch from me even my influenza.' All this time he was wondering about whether or not to go east. When he wrote to Brewster on 18 January he conceded 'for the first time' that Brewster might 'be right' and himself wrong. 'No, I believe you are right. Probably there, east, is the *source*: and America is the extreme periphery: Oh god, must one go to the extreme limit, then to come back?'

This might well be Rilke crying out. It almost sounds – the influence of Frieda? – as if it were translated from the German. Lawrence's reluctance to go east persisted but it was expressing itself less and less forcibly. 'I only know it seems so much *easier*, more peaceful to come east. But then peace, peace! I am *so* mistrustful of it: so much afraid that it means a sort of weakness and giving in.' A week later Lawrence gave in and arranged to go to Ceylon. He hated it, needless to say, and took what might be termed a profound personal dislike to Buddha 'and his rat-hole temples and his rat-hole religion'. Still, as he had said, he had gone east in order to go west, had seen the tranquillity of the east and could put it behind him. Brewster's way was not his. Rather, as he wrote to Rolf Gardiner, 'I am essentially a fighter – to wish me peace is bad luck – except the fighter's peace.'

And this fighter's peace *did* come to him. A new calm enters Lawrence's letters, from the beginning of 1926. It makes itself apparent not as an achieved or permanent state but as a tone. He had known interludes of repose before but, increasingly, the balance shifts towards contentment interspersed with outbreaks of rage. We must not sentimentalise Lawrence: again and again, especially when writing to the

Brewsters, he affirmed his fighter's nature – 'My business is a fight, and I've got to keep it up . . . Caro, don't ask me to pray for peace. I don't want it' – but he *was* becoming calmer. His philosophy remained fundamentally the same, namely that 'All truth – and real living is the only truth – has in it the elements of battle and repudiation. *Nothing is wholesale.* The problem of truth is: How can we most deeply *live?* And the answer is different in every case.' That, it seems to me, is the nearest Lawrence ever came to summing up all the diverse elements and contradictory impulses in his thought, in his life. In his own case, by 1926, living 'most deeply' meant becoming more accommodating, less unyielding.

This tendency towards accepting the world rather than railing against it was closely connected to the unavoidable fact of his own approaching death. In November 1929, writing to Brewster, he made a connection between his illness and his rage: 'But I do believe the root of all my sickness is a sort of rage. I realise now, Europe gets me into an awkward rage, that keeps my bronchials hellish inflamed.' Now that he was in the grips of his illness, now that he had accepted that he was ill, he could be at peace.

Again one must not exaggerate. Lawrence would have been horrified by the thought of 'mellowing'; rather he was in the condition evoked by Van Gogh in a letter to his brother, Theo: 'One no longer rebels against things, but neither is one resigned – one is ill and does not get better.' Perhaps Lawrence was close to the most difficult, elusively rewarding freedom of all: freedom from himself. He was still irritable and easily annoyed but there was an underlying calm and, as ever, Lawrence himself was aware of this. (Has anyone ever been more sensitive to the ebb and flow of their own feelings? Of course this is what he is famous for doing, through the characters in his novels, but I prefer the epistolary monologue to the drama of fiction.) 'For my part, though, I am perhaps *more* irascible being more easily irritable, not being well, still, I think I am more inwardly tolerant and companionable . . .'

Felicitous, that 'still'. Lawrence's calm was all the lovelier for the rage that had preceded it and it was expressed, again and again, in terms of stillness. At the beginning of his wandering he had remarked how he hated shifting; now, when shifting had become second nature, stillness became a measure of happiness. From Munich in 1927 he writes that it is 'very nice to be quite still: and this is one of the stillest places I know. The trees seem to make a silence. I really like it very much here, and I am honestly much better.' After all the gales of anger that had blown between them, he wrote to Ottoline Morrell, hoping that they might come to enjoy 'that stillness in friendship which is the best'.

'A fine wind is blowing the new direction of Time.' That was one of the first lines of Lawrence's that I read; the image that accompanied it, of Lawrence standing with the wind pouring through the sky, was one of the first images of him that I saw. At times this wind by which Lawrence lived threatened to tear him apart and this is why it is lovely to see him in his last years, gazing at the world as if it were a Matisse or Dufy, 'sitting in the sun and seeing the easy, drifting life of the place. That's how I am happiest nowadays – just sitting still, quite alone, with a little friendly life to watch.'

In the letters from the last years of Lawrence's life the realised ideal of stillness crops up again and again. It is like the ripe stillness preceding the autumn announced in his great poem 'The Ship of Death'. In the letters we have heard the pulse of that poem preparing itself for many years. Now there is a perceptible hush as the poem and the death which it anticipates begin, definitively, to grow in him. It is the combination of an achieved, contented mood and the increasing awareness of his own death that makes many of his letters from this period so heart-breaking: 'It is very lovely, the wind, the clouds, the running sea that bursts up like blossom on the island opposite. If only I was well, and had my strength back! But I am so weak. And something inside me weeps black tears. I wish it would go away.'

Let's return to that remark of Lawrence's about not wanting to let anyone filch even his influenza . . .

That Nietzsche had an influence on Lawrence is undoubted. Relying on an appalling travesty of Nietzsche's ideas, John Carey holds the philosopher responsible for most of the novelist's sillier ideas and his inclination towards a proto-fascist cult of the leader. The idea of the will to power certainly made an impact on Lawrence, and his reading of Nietzsche contributed, no doubt, to his distaste for democracy and his belief in a natural aristocracy or whatever nonsense it was he declared himself in favour of in the course of falling out with the aristocratic democrat Bertrand Russell. This, if you like, is first-order influence and I'm not concerned with it here.

But it is that remark about no one trying to filch from him his influenza that shows how at the level of his own life – and for Lawrence the 'struggle inside oneself' was 'the only history' that mattered – he had taken Nietzsche to heart. Not the ranting, posturing Nietzsche of *Zarathustra*, but, crucially, the Nietzsche of *The Gay Science* (which, rendered into French of a sort, became Lawrence's preferred title – 'Le Gai Savaire' – for his *Study of Thomas Hardy*).

In Camus too there is a direct philosophical debt to Nietzsche but, even more strikingly than in the case of Lawrence, it is an affinity of the soul that is all-important. Unlike Lawrence, Camus never flirted with the political extrapolations of Nietzsche's thought; instead, thinking specifically of the way in which Nietzsche's writings had been distorted to provide philosophical underpinning for Nazism, he wrote that we would 'never finish making reparation for the injustice done to' him.

There is something very moving about Lawrence and Camus – one the son of a miner, the other poor and fatherless – discovering Nietzsche: the former in Croydon Public Library in 1910, the latter in a textbook at the lycée in Algiers. Where Lawrence was inflamed by Nietzsche, Camus, as it were, took him for granted, finding in his writing the same 'intoxication' that he felt while walking in the sun of Algiers.[1] Algeria was a 'strange country' which gave the men it nourished 'both their wretchedness and their greatness'. During the summers there Camus learned that 'if there is a sin against life, it lies perhaps less in despairing of it than in hoping for another life, and evading the implacable grandeur of the one we have. These men have not cheated. They were gods of the summer at twenty in their thirst for life, and they are still gods today stripped of all hope.' He learned too that 'only one thing in life is more tragic than suffering, and that is the life of a happy man'. Testifying to the world that

---

[1] Rilke, too, writes of how he became 'slightly intoxicated' with Nietzsche.

formed and nourished him, Camus's essays celebrate the sensual embodiment of Nietzschean ideas. 'If the Greeks experienced despair,' writes Camus, 'it was always through beauty and its oppressive quality.' Camus strikes this note again and again ('there is no love of life without despair of life'); it is the same mood as that evoked by Nietzsche: 'in the most profound enjoyment of the moment, to be overcome by tears and the whole crimson melancholy of the happy'. This, according to Nietzsche, 'was the happiness of Homer' – and it is absolutely the mood of the young Camus.

Camus grew up in a world of poverty and sunlight, Lawrence in what Camus called 'the double damnation of poverty and ugliness'. But both – Lawrence blazing, defiantly, Camus calmly, lyrically – were not so much transformed as formed by Nietzsche.

I discovered Nietzsche in Brixton, in the mid-80s. Never to wish anything different, not now, not through all eternity: I can still remember the rush I felt on coming across that ideal of *amor fati*, absolute affirmation in the face of the Eternal Recurrence. My God! What an idea to live up to, what a challenge! As it happens I've ended up wishing *everything* different, now and through all eternity, but in my way I've stuck with it even though my way has involved regretting practically everything.

At school a teacher warned that if I spent all my time playing football and not studying then I would regret it in later life. As it happens I regret wasting so much time studying when I could have been playing football, but he almost had a point. What he should have said was that *whatever* you do you will regret it. A boy at school, Paul Hynes, was nearer the mark when, as part of his pre-scrap intimidation, he threatened: 'You do that and you'll regret it.' I did and I did. *You'll regret it*: there are worse mottoes to live by. Successful people say that it is stupid to regret things but the futility of regret only increases its power. Even while regretting things you're consumed with regret about doing so. Looking back, the tiniest regrets weigh heavily on me: the time I bought a Weekly Travel Pass and fell fifty pence short of breaking even; the day in February when I was too miserly to pay seventy-nine francs for a rare Yma Sumac CD which, when I went back to buy it two days later, had disappeared. Even now, ten months later, I can't stop thinking about that Yma Sumac CD: I wish I'd bought it when I had the chance but since I didn't buy it when I had the chance I wish I'd never seen it in the first place because then I wouldn't be tormented by the thought that I *could* have bought it – but the reason I didn't buy it, of course, is because I was thinking of how much I'd regretted buying my last Yma Sumac CD which turned out to be not worth buying . . . Looking back through my diary is like reading a vast anthology of regret and squandered opportunity. Oh well, I find myself thinking, life is there to be wasted.

But this is an affirmative way of living. I accept the consequences of doing things which I will later regret. In a sense then I regret them before I do them. Instead of resolving to learn to cook I regret to inform myself that by the end of the year I will still not know how to cook (because I hate cooking) even though learning to cook would improve my life no end. Instead of doing the exercises which will save my right knee – and I will say more about my knees in a moment – I resign myself to regretting not having done something about what will, in a few years, be a debilitating, potentially crippling ailment. I resign myself to things: this is my own warped version of *amor fati*: regretting everything but resigning myself to this regret. However things turn out I am bound to wish they had turned out differently. I am resigned to that.

Take this book which is intermittently about Lawrence. Right now I profoundly regret ever having started it. I wish I hadn't bothered. But if I hadn't started it I would have regretted not having done so. I knew this and so I got on with it and now that I have got on with it I regret that I got on with it in the way I did. I regret that it will not turn out to be the sober, academic study of Lawrence that I had hoped to write but I accept this because I know that, in the future, when it is finished, I won't want it to be any different. I'll be glad that this little book turned out how it did because I will see that what was intended to be a sober, academic study of D. H. Lawrence had to become a case history. Not a history of how I *recovered* from a breakdown but of how breaking down became a means of continuing. Anyone can have a breakdown, anyone. The trick is to have a breakdown and take it in one's stride. Ideally one would get to the stage where one had a total nervous breakdown and didn't even notice. That, I realise now, is the lesson learned last winter after our abortive trip to Mexico, to 'beastly Oaxaca'.

What sticks in my mind about Oaxaca is how little I remember of it. We were on the Lawrence trail, of course, but already, even by that stage, the borders of the Lawrence trail were so vaguely defined that it was difficult to imagine an activity *not* undertaken with Lawrence in mind, that could not be justified by appeal to his name. I thought back to the

Blue Line Trail in Eastwood, that narrow strip of paint taking the visitor on an efficient, carefully chosen stroll from one Lawrence-related place to another. My so-called Lawrence trail, on the other hand, was fast becoming unrecognisable, identified, if at all, by its lack of direction, by its overwhelming purposelessness, its capacity to encompass any and every detour. And yet I felt a determination to stick with it, to stick with the peculiarities of a path determined less by Lawrence than by an unswerving fidelity to the vagaries of my nature. By *straying*, I liked to think, I was following Lawrence's directions to the letter.

In retrospect it seems now that we went to Oaxaca simply to find a doctor for Laura who had fallen ill. We had quarrelled over some tuna steaks in Puerto Angel. The waiter assured us that the fish on the menu was not tuna. We ordered it and it *was* tuna, needless to say, a fish I detest more than all the other kinds of fish which I also detest but which, unlike tuna, I *will* eat if pushed. Tuna, though, I *cannot* eat and so I refused to taste even a mouthful since not only was this fish clearly tuna it was also a particularly revolting-looking tuna which Laura, in protest against my indignation, insisted on eating with relish. I stormed off to eat something marginally less revolting, and that was – or should have been – that.

It was a sad end to what had been an interesting day, to say the least, the culmination of what might be termed our *oceanic* experiences. We had spent the day in Zipolite, getting wasted. The name, Zipolite, means something to do with Death. It's a strip of beach a mile long. There are no hotels, just a few *palapas* offering beer, shade, and, if you are staying the night, a place to hang your hammock. It is possible to buy grass there and we had done so the day before, missing the last bus to Puerto Angel and walking back along the dirt road in the moonlit darkness. As far as I could make out it was never not a full moon in this part of the world. The grass was terribly strong and everyone in Zipolite was high the whole time. Naked too. To call it a nudist beach, however, is to dress it up in too many words. People say they feel naked without a favourite item of clothing. Here, so to speak, they felt naked without nothing on. The effect of this, as far as I could make out, was the opposite of what allegedly occurs in nudist camps: the de-eroticisation of nakedness. In Zipolite we were horny as rabbits all day. We had sex on the brain. Primitive, hair-pulling sex. Clothesless sex, naked sex. Also, like all women, Laura is completely at ease without her clothes, and felt quite at home naked on the beach at Zipolite. I couldn't get used to it. I am not really comfortable in shorts, let alone swimming trunks, let alone naked. And despite all the sun worship in his writing it is difficult to imagine Lawrence being happy without his clothes on. Easier to think of him trussed up in his tweed jacket, not wanting anyone to see his scrawny chest, clothing his embarrassment by sneering about the philosopher in *his* swimming costume: 'Poor Bertie Russell! He's all disembodied mind!' Or – as in a photograph of Lawrence and Huxley – drawing his knees up to his chest, wrapping his hands around his knees so that his sleeves become a blanket, hiding the thin trunk the arms are joined to.

We are skinny, narrow-shouldered men, Lawrence and I. As a teenager I was so ashamed of my skinny legs that I played squash in jeans. Even before that, when I was a boy, I avoided wearing shinpads while playing football because, I felt, the bulk added to my shins and made my thighs seem even scrawnier. My father kept saying I would thicken out but I never did, never will. By the time I am fifty I will be one of those men with narrow shoulders and a droopy, kangaroo paunch. There was a time though, I found myself thinking as I sat naked, smoking dope on the beach at Zipolite, when, in my early thirties, I'd had strong shoulders, when I'd believed that you could not know what it meant to be a man unless you had strong shoulders and arms. Then, after a few years of pumping iron, my shoulders gradually reverted to their Cluedo-piece norm – but I have never quite shaken off the conviction that I was more of a man in that brief period than I was before or have been since. It was a good feeling, I reflected on the beach at Zipolite. Women like men with broad shoulders, men like my friend Trevor, for example, whose girlfriend I have often wanted to sleep with but whom I would never dream of sleeping with – whom I dream of sleeping with all the time but only dare *dream* of sleeping with – because I am always embarrassed at the thought of her seeing and feeling my bony shoulders and wishing they were more like Trevor's. Lawrence may have claimed that there was more to being a man than manliness, more to being a man, in other words, than having broad shoulders, but, equally, there is more to being broadshouldered than having broad shoulders. The metaphorical connotations of having a broad back – of being able to endure things, of being resilient – are qualities by which Lawrence set considerable store. For my part, I thought to myself on the beach at Zipolite, even more than broad shoulders, I would like to have had the qualities of broadshoulderedness but, metaphorically too, I am, as they say, a narrow-shouldered, long-necked kind of guy: incapable of enduring anything, lacking in resilience, weak, prone to sudden eruptions of temper over petty hindrances. 'To be brave, to keep one's word, to be generous': this, for Lawrence, was what it meant to be a man. The narrator of Berger's story 'Once in Europa' says something similar. According to her the men who deserve women's respect are 'men who give themselves to hard labour so that those close to them can eat. Men who are generous with everything they own. And men who spend their lives looking for God. The rest are pigshit.' I loved that even more than I loved Lawrence's version, even though it meant I was not a man who deserved respect, was pigshit, in fact. I do no work, I am mean with everything I own and . . . and the more I thought about it the worse I felt.

'I am so wound up in myself I am not even a man,' I said to Laura, suddenly on the brink of tears.

'Yes you are, *hombre*,' said Laura.

It would have been okay, I thought, if I had been here six or seven years ago when I was pumping iron, but now my nudity seemed to reveal the narrow shoulders which my swimming trunks contrived somehow to conceal. My swimming trunks padded out my shoulders. If I felt uncomfortable with no clothes on, however, I felt even more uncomfortable in my swimming trunks because they chafed somewhat so that I was actually more comfortable with no clothes on. Lying down was okay but when I stood up on my Bambi legs, naked, the idea of wearing chafing swimming trunks, even swimming trunks that chafed my skinny legs terribly, seemed preferable to standing there naked, skinny shoulders revealed for all the world to see. It was like this, being stoned at

Zipolite: it was very good grass but you could easily find yourself drawn into a whirlpool of anxiety. To avoid being sucked under, engulfed by anxiety, I moved around in front of Laura who was dozing, one knee raised up, legs slightly apart so that I could see her cunt. After a few moments I became lost in the pleasure of looking at her breasts, her legs, her stomach, her cunt. My prick stirred into life. I thought of lying between her legs and licking her clitoris while she pissed, her piss running over my chin and immediately sizzling into the sand and disappearing. My prick became hard. I spat in my hand and rubbed saliva over the head of my prick – stopping abruptly when I realised that I was sitting on the beach at Zipolite with a semi-hard-on, right on the brink of masturbating, an activity which, to put it mildly, emphasised my nakedness and, therefore, my narrow-shoulderedness which was exactly what I had hoped to take my mind off by gazing at Laura's cunt. Besides, grains of sand were stuck in the palm of my hand and, even allowing for the lubricating effects of saliva, what I would have been doing would have been subjecting my prick to a form of highly animated chafing: mastur-chafing, as it were. I turned around, away from Laura, and stared at the ocean, letting my prick soften.

The ocean. Now that I was facing it I became conscious again of the motorway roar and crash of tide. Big thoughts were in order. The waves were huge: blue-white walls rearing up and pounding the beach. A couple of perfect Germans walked along the damp sand at the water's edge, a man and woman, naked, both with the same broad-shoulder-length hair, holding hands, taking it in turns to pull on a joint. It was paradise in a way, Zipolite: Anarcho-Eden-on-sea. You could probably fuck here, on the beach, in blazing daylight, and no one would bat an eyelid. The only thing you couldn't do, if you came across people doing that, was what you most wanted to do: watch.

There were pelicans flying over the sea, a few people swimming. I stood up and walked towards the sea. The sand burned my feet and I ran towards the damp sand at the water's edge where the footprints of the perfect Germans were already disappearing. The sea was spiteful as fat in a pan: I went in up to my knees and was almost bowled over by the waves. The undertow wrenched the sand from beneath my feet like someone tugging a rug. The sea was trying to tear everything back into itself, making a bid for Zipolite itself, trying to haul it back into the sea grain by grain.

Out where the Berlin Wall waves were crashing in, two people were swimming. However you chose to look at it they were having a huge dose of ocean. They were emphatically not paddling. Toppling over the crest of one of those waves was like falling off a cliff – and then having the cliff come crashing over on top of you.

They started coming back in, swimming together. I could see them more clearly now: a man and a woman. A wave crashed over them and he held her up above the waves. I was the only other person around, in the water up to my thighs, surrounded by the hiss and foam, the roar. They had their arms around each other but as they came nearer I saw that she was out on her feet, head lolling. Not only that but she was pale green. As I watched, her knees buckled and she collapsed. The guy picked her up in his arms: a classic example of broad-shouldered behaviour. Someone else came splashing out beside me, the waves thumping into us. It was a French guy Laura and I had spoken to the day before – and the woman, I realised now, was his girlfriend.

We waded out a little further. Then the guy who'd saved her – evidently – and the French boyfriend walked back into the shallows with the woman sagging between them. There was nothing for me to do except watch as the French boyfriend and some other Europeans led the woman back up the beach. After that, I walked with the guy who'd saved her back along the beach, puppy waves snapping at our ankles.

'I saw you out there. I thought you were messing around,' I said, wanting to hear all about it, wanting the full story.

He'd been standing some way off – he was Australian – trying to figure out the rips. Ocean people do this, they figure out the rips. He'd seen her get hit by a wave, seen her go under. As soon as she came up she got hit by another. She didn't know where she was. Waves kept smacking into her and she was getting pulled out to sea. He swam out to her but it looked like he'd got there too late. He thought she was dead but as soon as he touched her she pulled him under. He wrestled himself free, kept hold of her, rode the waves in. Saved her.

'You must be a good swimmer,' I said.

In the circumstances it was a stupid remark but he nodded and said, 'I grew up by the ocean.' The fact that we were walking, naked, by the edge of the ocean helped imbue this reply with an elemental appropriateness, yes, but wherever we were I would have liked the suggestion of dues paid, of a long apprenticeship of the waves. I would also have liked the way that he didn't specify which ocean, as if there was only one ocean. Also, the romanticism of growing up *by* something: the railroad tracks, the gasworks, the North Circular even.

The Australian walked back to the bar. 'I need a drink after that,' he said.

'You deserve one,' I said and hurried back to wake Laura, to tell her I'd seen someone plucked from death's watery embrace. She was still sleepy, disoriented. Some way over to our right a group was forming round the French couple. I put on my chafing trunks. The French couple's friends were trying to administer some kind of first aid but they didn't really know what they were doing. The boyfriend tried the kiss of life, a muscular German manipulated her arms as if she were a rowing machine. A bald guy said she should sit up; an Italian tried to manoeuvre her into the coma position. From where I was standing it looked more like a gang-rape than an attempt to save her life. No one knew what to do.

No one except the Australian, who touched me on the elbow and walked over. He too had put on some swimming trunks. He walked slowly over the hot sand and took control of the situation. That's exactly what a situation is, I thought to myself, something someone will take control of. Implicit in the idea of a situation is someone taking control of it. Quickly he made her puke up a lot of water, reassured her, told someone to get a doctor.

I went back to where Laura was lying, sitting up now. She put on her bikini bottom and we walked over to the bar. After a while the Australian came over with his group of friends. They ordered beers and he told the story again. I chipped in from time to time.

'She OD'd on the ocean, man,' said a guy from

California who had seen everything many times before.

'The waves were too much for her,' said the Australian, shaking his head. I realised we both had towels round our necks. I was only a witness but the gravity of the situation had invested me with a certain authority in everyone's eyes.

I put down my beer like a judge pounding his gavel, clutched the ends of my towel with both hands and said, 'You've got to respect the ocean.'

'You said it man. What's your name anyway?' said the Californian, reaching out his hand.

'Call him Ishmael,' said Laura. 'Ishmael or Hombre.'

We hung out with our new friends for the rest of the day and then, in the evening, back in Puerto Angel, we had the quarrel about our tuna steaks. Laura fell ill the next day. She had a fever and terrible diarrhoea and spent the whole day lying on her bed in the hotel where major renovations were taking place. We were woken at six by the incredible sound of birds; once that had died down the drilling started. I went to the beach with my mask and snorkel but the water was too murky to see anything. The sun was too hot. I could feel it piercing my skin, doing damage. It has changed since Lawrence's time, the sun. Then it healed, now it harms. I looked down sometimes and was surprised that I cast a shadow: the sun was hot enough to go straight through me and dissolve shadows. I had been in hot places before, I like hot places, but I had never been anywhere as hot as this. Even though, technically, I had been in places that were maybe a few degrees hotter, I had never been anywhere that felt as hot as here – except Rome perhaps. Who knows? There's something about the heat, in places that are seriously hot, that compels you to think not in relative but in absolute terms. One lives in a perpetual, boiling present. Even people who have lived in hot places all their lives, whose families have lived there for generations, feel compelled to comment on how hot it is, as though they have never felt anything like it. In a seriously hot place, somewhere where temperatures coagulate for six months a year in the nineties, people are commenting in astonished, resigned tones about the heat every ten minutes. Eventually that is all you do: you wipe your forehead and say how hot it is. Entire summers can pass like this. Apart from the heat, nothing else happens. The heat is the only news. For some peoples the sum total of their destiny is to mop their foreheads and remark on the heat. A good life, I think, one unclouded by culture. The sun beats down. Only the angles change. One moment you are young – a boy in shorts and T-shirt, or a girl barefoot, in sandals – the next you are ancient, worn out and widowed, but that moment lasts at least one lifetime, usually several.

When it became too hot – which was all the time – I went back to find Laura on her bed, shivering and sweating, her ears plugged with cotton wool to keep the drilling at bay. People often fall ill in Mexico, I thought to myself, you expect to fall ill in Mexico, you *go* to Mexico to get ill. Lawrence became incredibly ill in Mexico ('malaria – with grippe – and typhoid') and now Laura was incredibly ill. I wasn't ill but I felt strange: disoriented, exhausted. It was too hot and I was not used to smoking such strong grass. I had nothing to read except *The Plumed Serpent*: an interesting case of the site-specific book which you bring to read because it is set in the place you are visiting but which you cannot bear to read. There are people who can read anything to pass the time, and our situation should have forced me to read *The Plumed Serpent* but I simply could not bear to. I preferred to stare into space. Laura lay on her bed. The French guy whose girlfriend had almost drowned told us there was a good doctor in Oaxaca, and we decided to take a bus there, to 'beastly Oaxaca' as Lawrence called it, not because we had any particular desire to seek medical assistance – the difference between being ill and being in robust health was becoming increasingly hazy – but because we felt the need to do something, to assert ourselves, to prove that we still had the capacity to act, to play a part.

Laura was too weak even to pack and so, grumbling and muttering under my breath, I got all our stuff together. I wrapped up the grass and stored it in my glasses case and then, still muttering and grumbling, lugged our bags to the bus station. It felt good to be on the move even though it felt terrible to be on the bus again. We had spent too long on buses and it is possible that although it was the tuna steaks that did for Laura it was the interminable bus journeys that softened her up, weakened her resistance to the point where a mere tuna steak was enough to finish her off. We had made terrible mistakes. The whole of our Mexico trip, it seems to me now, looking back, was a terrible mistake. We crossed the border at Tijuana which was a mistake: we should have flown to Oaxaca direct instead of crossing the border at Tijuana and then taking a bus right down Baja California where there was nothing to see for hundreds and hundreds of miles. Even if we had crossed the border at Tijuana instead of flying to Oaxaca, even if we had made that mistake, we should have caught a train in Tijuana or taken a bus down to Los Mochis not, as we did, compounding our mistake by travelling all the way down Baja California where there is nothing to see for hundreds and hundreds of miles. Never reinforce failure: that is the first rule of military strategy. But we kept reinforcing our failure, kept taking buses that nudged us towards Oaxaca, rather than cutting our losses and flying straight there. We caught a ferry at La Paz, a vile ferry that left us so exhausted that when we arrived at Mazatlán we were too tired to think and got straight on a bus to Guadalajara. We kept pressing on, taking more and more buses, getting more and more exhausted. The longer we spent on buses, the less significant each additional instalment of the journey by bus seemed. How long would the bus take from Guadalajara to Mexico City? Eight hours? Eight hours was nothing. Two tickets please. And so it went on until it seemed that all our experience of Mexico would amount to was peering out of bus windows. One says Mexico, one means a bus. Finally we could take it no more. We arrived in Mexico City, took a bus to the airport and got on the first plane to Puerto Escondido.

Originally the idea had been to go to Oaxaca, to seek out Lawrence-related places, and then spend a week chilling in one of the Puertos – Escondido or Angel – before heading up to New Mexico, to Taos, to resume our Lawrence research. Instead, after weeks on buses, we flew straight to Puerto Escondido which we then left, on a bus, to go to Oaxaca, where we should have flown in the first place.

Just outside Escondido the bus slowed at an army checkpoint. Teenage soldiers had pulled over another coach and hauled everyone out, were going through everything, looking for arms and drugs. It was impossible to think of a more foolish place to keep drugs than in a metal spectacles case which would clatter and flash if thrown out of the window. Always keep drugs in your underpants: that is one of my mottoes in life. Better safe than sorry, that is another. A soldier peered in through the window and waved us on.

The road became a knot tying and untying itself. The bus twisted around curves, looming over the edge of ravines at the bottom of which could be seen the charred wrecks of many other buses. One says Mexico, one means yet another bus in Mexico, swathing round bends.

On the outskirts of Oaxaca we slowed at another checkpoint. Stopped. A soldier boarded the bus which fell immediately silent. Walked down the aisle, letting the fear spread out in front of him like sweat patches on a shirt. 'This is it,' I kept saying to myself, over and over, 'this is it.' I felt resigned. There was nothing I could do. I was close to that moment of total liberation which – or so I had read – comes with arrest, when you abandon all claim to being an active participant in your own destiny. For this reason I looked completely calm. The boy-soldier said something mildly threatening to a woman just a few seats ahead of me. Walked on. Then, carbine still pointed to the floor, he raised his eyes, looked at me. Stood there and waited. I looked back at him. He was clean-shaven, possibly had not even begun to shave. His fatigues were damp beneath his arms.

'*Pasaporte, por favor,*' he said. To get at my passport I had to stand up which was difficult to do without banging my head on the luggage rack – so I stood up *very* quickly, as if eager to obey, and smashed my head on the sag of cases – not hard enough to hurt myself, just to look ridiculous – and crumpled lankily back into my seat. The woman next to me laughed. The soldier laughed. I rubbed my head, *not* making a meal of it. Stood up more gently. Handed him the passport which he looked at kindly.

'*Cuidado*,' he said, handing back the passport and pointing to the luggage rack. 'Careful.'

'*Sí*,' I said, not smiling. '*Gracias*.' The soldier walked back down the aisle, said something to the driver who said something back and they both laughed. Then he got off the bus and waved us on. As the bus rumbled into motion again I had half a mind to open my spectacles case and give the boy-soldier a flash of its fragrant, delirium-inducing contents.

I look back on this as one of the two or three incidents which prove how far I have come in the quest for wisdom. I rank it alongside the time in France when I was on the brink of buying a shirt which was only just big enough, which the assistant assured me would not shrink, but which I *knew* would shrink (less wisely, I bought it anyway). The episode on the bus confirmed what I had long suspected: the massive advantages of appearing ridiculous. Only those with dignity can ever lose it. Whereas I, ever since that moment on the bus, have behaved with no dignity whatsoever. I can walk down a street in my best clothes and fall flat on my face with no appreciable loss of dignity because I am someone who is, in some sense, already flat on his face, already devoid of dignity.

As soon as we arrived in Oaxaca we took a taxi to see the doctor, a tall American who did not look in the best of health himself. Laura had an amoeba, he explained, and a fever known as 'the breaker'. In Laura's fever-dulled eyes there was a brief flicker of pride that what she was suffering from merited so terrible a name. Who knows what she was feeling? Like flu only worse, I suppose. He gave us antibiotics and we checked into a hotel, a nice place run by a family who were always eager to help.

Even when the antibiotics had begun working Laura felt too weak to walk. I sniffed around the city a little but my heart wasn't in it. How often I find myself using this phrase as I get older: my heart wasn't in it, my heart isn't in it. Maybe those are the words that should be on my grave: 'His heart wasn't in it.' I should have sought out Lawrence-related places but my heart wasn't in it. I was suffering one of those strange losses of purpose that come over one from time to time, that had come over me, in very mild form, in the Lawrence Birthplace Museum in Eastwood. Right on the brink of doing that which you came to do, close to achieving some long-anticipated wish, suddenly you lose interest. It always happens to me before parties. Even if I have looked forward to a party for months, even if I have enjoyed the process of choosing what to wear, still, at some point, minutes before arriving, I find I want to do nothing so much as return home, to stay in and watch TV. It's not a question of dread or social anxiety, but a strange becalming that leaves one stranded, inert. It happened in Cairo when only a fantastic effort of will dragged me from my hotel to the pyramids which were the things in Egypt I most wanted to see, and in Moscow when I only just managed to get to the Pushkin Museum to see the Gauguins that I had waited years to see. It had happened many, many times but never so catastrophically as in Oaxaca. We had come all this way in Lawrence's footsteps. We weren't there to do research, to consult dusty, non-existent archives but still, had it not been for Lawrence we would not have come to Mexico at all; at the very least Lawrence provided the incentive to travel to Mexico, a country I had never had any real *desire* to visit – and now that we were here, in Oaxaca, a town that was fairly important for Lawrence, I found that I not only had no impulse to seek out the places he had stayed, but was actually incapable of forcing myself – as I had forced myself to see the pyramids and the Gauguins – to seek out these places, places where he had written parts of *The Plumed Serpent*, a novel which I could not bring myself to read. Not only did I not read *The Plumed Serpent* but, I find now, I do not like to even think about *The Plumed Serpent* because it reminds me of that non-time in beastly Oaxaca.

What *did* I do in beastly Oaxaca? Moped around the hotel, brought Laura glasses of water, asked how she was feeling, hung out in the zócola, went to the market at Central de Abastos and negotiated the purchase of a hammock which I didn't get round to buying. Killed time, hung out in the zócola, concentrated on not getting ill even though, looking back, it seems to me now that I *was* in the grip of some illness which was all the more malign for being apparently symptomless. Laura and I discussed what to do, which actually meant discussing what not to do. We decided not to stay in Mexico and not to bother with New Mexico either. All Laura wanted to do was get back home, to Italy, to Rome. I didn't care what I did so we agreed to fly back to Rome. It was all the same to me. I was becoming indifferent to everything, a feeling which turned out to be an intimation of the deep depression I would sink into back in Rome and which I will talk about later.

This depression was compounded by the way that, back

in Rome, I was aghast that I could have squandered my time in Oaxaca so thoroughly. I flung myself into whatever books about Lawrence were around, doing the research retrospectively that should have preceded our trip to Mexico, checking Lawrence's movements, discovering that he stayed at the Hotel Francia ('very pleasant') and then rented a house at 43 Avenida Pino Suarez ('very beautiful'). There was such an abundance of information on Lawrence in Oaxaca it even seemed, for a brief moment, that I could, as it were, overdub my visit to Oaxaca. This hope proved futile. All this frenzied activity was really just a kind of twitching, some last fizzle of energy before I succumbed to terrible depression.

Looking back on our abortive trip to Oaxaca now, writing about our abortive trip to Oaxaca, I am still surprised that I squandered my time there so thoroughly. Although it had been easy to discover that Lawrence stayed at the Hotel Francia it was more difficult to find where we had stayed for a week. A parrot filled the leaf-soaked courtyard with blue and green squawking, I remember that, but I kept no notes, have no record of the name of the place. I've looked at the *Rough Guide* and *Let's Go* but can't find anything that jogs my memory. It is no use; it is gone, lost. Long resigned to lacking the application adequately to research Lawrence's life I find I am not even qualified to research my own, to be my own biographer.

If one could accept one's own shortcomings, perhaps one could be happy, contented, at one, as they say, with oneself; but what if one's principal shortcoming is, precisely, this unlimited capacity to generate friction between giving in to oneself as one is one moment and the equally strong urge to re-shape and seize control of how one *was* at some later date? Nothing wrong *per se* in going to Oaxaca and deciding, once you are there, that you do not want to do exactly that which you came to do. It might even be tolerable to fail to do what you came to do and to come to regret it later, but to fail to do something now precisely so that you can gnaw and gnaw away at it later, and then to waste weeks gnawing over this syndrome . . . No, there is not even the glimmer of contentment there. You're stuck, stuck in an endless loop, stuck like a record which keeps jumping back to the same three words – 'if only . . .', 'if only . . .' – which turn out to be only two words.

In Oaxaca, I thought to myself in Rome, I did not accomplish what I set out to accomplish. Fine, fine. Except I could not accept that, could not abide by the consequences of that failure. The only way I could rectify things, it seemed, was to leave Rome immediately, to set out for Oaxaca on the first available plane. That was the only possible course of action. That is what I will do, I said to myself. I will go to Oaxaca. Immediately. But, equally, even as I was filled with the power of this implacable resolution to make good my previous mistake, I knew that I would *not* go to Oaxaca again, that I had no intention of going to Oaxaca, that of all the places on earth I might return to, Oaxaca was not one of them, that this determination to go back to Oaxaca was actually a way of coming to terms with *not* going to Oaxaca, was a way of atoning for my earlier failure by compounding it.

And out of *this*, it seems to me now, out of compound failures like these, comes a kind of contentment. I cannot accept myself as I am but, ultimately, I am resigned to accepting this inability to accept myself as I am. Anything, anything – as long as it doesn't involve the slightest effort or inconvenience. 'Let a man go to the bottom of what he *is*,' wrote Lawrence, 'and believe in that.'

Still, however bad I felt after Oaxaca and however ill Laura had been, it was nothing compared with the state Lawrence got himself into. *He* left Oaxaca 'a mere wreck'. By then, though, he must have been used to feeling like this, to feeling 'seedy' the whole time, to being laid up in bed and plagued, even in interludes of relatively good health, by colds and coughs.

Imagine being Lawrence, imagine being ill like that. I can't imagine anything worse. I dread being ill. I live in terror of it. One of the symptoms, in fact, of this symptomless illness I have decided I am suffering from is a pathological dread of getting ill, a phantom hypochondria: I haven't had a cold for over a year now and the longer I go without getting one the more dreadful the prospect becomes. But how can you avoid getting a cold, I often find myself thinking, when everyone else has one? Talk about sick office, or sick building syndrome: most cities suffer from sick city syndrome. London is the worst. Lawrence realised this in 1916: London was 'so foul', he reckoned, that 'one would die in it in a fortnight'. Since then it's got even worse. Now it's the world capital of flu. The sky in London drizzles flu, it rains flu. People from all over the world go there and get flu. Whether they come to see the changing of the guard, or to take ecstasy at raves, they all end up getting flu. Those who work in London are all either going down with flu, recovering from flu, or in the grip of flu – even though most of the people going down with flu, recovering from flu or in the grip of flu don't have flu at all. What they're actually suffering from is verbal inflation because no one says they have a cold any more, it's always flu. If people have a cold they say they have flu; if they say they have a cold it means there's nothing wrong with them. Flu and cold are becoming interchangeable. We say flu when we mean cold but we say flu when we mean flu because no one wants to say they have pneumonia when all they've got is flu because if you say you have pneumonia people might think you have AIDS. It's even possible that people who *do* have pneumonia call it flu so that flu now runs the whole gamut of illness from the common cold upwards. To say we have flu is merely to express the common condition of urban life at the tail-end of the twentieth century. One way or another we all have flu all the time, even during those periods when we are, to all intents and purposes, in perfect health. Seen in a certain light there's barely a moment in the year when we don't have flu.

Having said that, *I* haven't had a cold or flu for over a year. Not a sniffle. Why? Because I don't have a job or children. If I had followed through with my intention of getting a job in Dullford I would have had at least four colds in the last year and if I had children it could easily have been double that number. Offices are places of contagion and so are schools. People in offices and parents with children catch colds all the time. These are facts. There is a whole array of new viruses going around the playgrounds now, different ones to the ones that were going round when we were at school and to which, over the years, we have developed immunity. Children bring these new viruses home from school and adults have no immunity against them. Stay away from children and stay away from parents who become infected by their children's germs. Take evasive action. Stay away from everyone if necessary. Even talking on the phone is risky. There are cases of people catching virulent strains of flu over the telephone. Still, better to get flu than become a germ paranoiac, a germ recluse. Only by going out into the world can you build up resistance to it. By staying in, by keeping away from schools and offices, you actually become more prone to infection, more likely to go down with flu. Better to get out in the world, better to board a train full of sniffers, sneezers and coughers, even if it entails a young woman sitting diagonally opposite you, full up with a cold: sniffling, her eyes all glazed and watery, feeling terrible, blowing her nose in used tissues. My first impulse was to change seats but I thought this might be rude, and because I was worried about appearing rude I became angry that this woman had put me in the awkward position whereby I had either to behave rudely or risk infection. Besides, I thought, I was here before her, I posed no risk to my fellow-passengers' health, why should I move? If anyone was going to move it would be her, not me. I was going to sit here no matter what. The more I thought about it the more it seemed not simply an act of gross selfishness that she had chosen to sit where she had, but actually an outrage that British Rail had permitted her to travel and risk infecting other paying customers with what was clearly a virulent strain of flu. I thought these thoughts in a semi-formalised way, almost as if composing a draft letter of complaint to the customer services manager. Even as I resolved to stay put I decided to move to a different seat but as soon as I made up my mind to move I saw there were no empty seats so that I was now faced with an even starker choice: either I could stay where I was and catch a virulent strain of flu or I could stand. I had no intention of standing, obviously, so I forced myself deep into my seat and read the paper (full, incidentally, of graphic expressionist advertisements for cold and flu cures), using it as a shield and consoling myself with the thought that actually this was quite a good seat because I was facing backwards, was ahead of the woman opposite me, so that, as she exhaled, her germs were taken back down the train. The more I dwelt on this the more I seemed to be in a good position because the person most at risk from her germs was probably the person sitting down-wind, down-train, from her, oblivious to the contagion that lurked nearby, whereas I was relatively safe and could, metaphorically speaking, keep an eye on her from behind my paper while preparing my defences, steeling my immune system against possible assault. No sooner had I thought this than I realised that for all I knew there was someone up-train from me, suffering from an even more virulent strain of flu, blowing his or her germs back towards me. In fact this seemed not just probable but highly likely since the train was full of the sound of sneezing, coughing, nose blowing and sniffling. The clack of the wheels was all but lost beneath the sound of sniffling, sneezing, coughing and nose blowing. As far as I could make out I was actually the only person on the train who was not sneezing, sniffling, nose blowing or coughing. Everyone else was practically dying of flu, the air was full of bits of mucus-soaked Kleenex that had floated off from over-used packs of tissue. It was like being on a hospital train during the great flu epidemic of 1919 . . . My own breathing was becoming laboured, stuffy – I woke up with a jolt, the

Guardian shrouding my face, semi-suffocated by newsprint. The woman opposite me was still there, pestilential, sniffling. The train had stopped suddenly in the middle of the dark countryside. There was a house with lights on, surrounded by endemic darkness.

As we sat there, waiting for the train to move, it occurred to me that being illness-free was probably a form of compensation for being so ailment- and injury-prone. Ailments: the myriad minor malfunctions and mechanical failings the flesh is heir to. Sensitive skin, for example. I have extremely sensitive skin. I don't know anyone whose skin is as sensitive as mine. I am allergic to everything, even those hyper-allergenic products *designed* for sensitive skin. As a child I had terrible eczema. As an adult my eczema is either getting better or worse depending on your point of view. I am no longer prone to the terrible attacks of eczema which used to leave my fingers unusably brittle. Seen in this light my eczema has improved. On the other hand, mild eczema has spread to parts of the body never previously affected (behind my knees, for example, on my neck and forearms, on my feet and around my eyelids) and the general health of my skin has deteriorated to the extent that there is no longer a sharp distinction between the parts of the body which are eczema-free and those which are eczema-afflicted. If I no longer notice eczema on my fingers that is partly because, in a sense, I am covered in eczema from head to foot. My skin is so dry that I might as well treat my whole body as if it had eczema since any attempt to alleviate my dry skin by moisturisers almost inevitably leads to an outbreak of eczema. I am allergic to bath oils. I am, in short, a man who can never fill his bathroom with sweet-smelling, strawberry-coloured lotions from The Body Shop. Other men my age use their bathroom shelves to display a range of seductive-smelling, fruit-coloured lotions which can also be used for erotic massages but I keep tubes of prescription-only ointments hidden in a bathroom cabinet along with Anusol and Canesten. My idea of sensual bliss would be to lie, Marat-style, in a bath full of warm Betnovate, the cortisone ointment one can use only sparingly because it ruins the skin, apparently; even as it repairs, it ruins, as it heals it destroys.

The train was still stuck in the darkness. My fellow passengers were becoming anxious but I was thinking about how, when I contracted athlete's foot recently, my various skin disorders became so intermingled it was difficult to say which bits of the body were suffering from which ailments. I contracted athlete's foot, that much is clear. I then began to suffer from a mild itchiness between my fingers, an itchiness so similar to the itchiness between my toes that it seemed to me that I was suffering from athlete's hand. Logically enough I began to treat my athlete's hand with my athlete's foot cream – only to find, or so my doctor explained, that the athlete's foot cream set off a terrible reaction in my hand which led to the original itchiness being consumed by an appalling outbreak of eczema.

'Let me make sure I understand this,' I said to the doctor who outlined the origins of this sudden rash of skin trouble. 'What you are saying, effectively, is that I am allergic to athlete's foot.'

'Effectively, yes,' said the doctor.

Then there are my knees. Oh, don't get me on my knees. What's wrong with my knee? Everything. Everything that can go wrong with a knee has gone wrong with mine.

Muscle, bone, cartilage, tendon. My knee exists in a bewildering variety of hurt: the pain is throbbing, aching, stabbing, dull, acute. Where does it hurt? Above the kneecap, to the side of it, below it, and *in* the knee-cap. Oh my poor knee. *Knees*, I should say. Plural. Both knees are in bad shape but it's the right that takes the biscuit. I waited for years to have something done about it, about them, because with all of this moving around I was doing I was never in a position to seek sustained medical treatment. In New Orleans I happened to make the acquaintance of a knee specialist who diagnosed *chondro malacia* of the patella. He recommended strength-building exercises which I did for two days and then gave up. Since then I've been waiting for my life to stabilise sufficiently to seek serious, sustained medical treatment. As soon as I moved to Dullford I registered with a doctor who made an appointment with the knee specialist. Six months later, the big day: my meeting with the knee specialist, a tall man with a perceptible limp. I'm sure it comes from having played too much squash in my late twenties and early thirties, I said. I played squash for eight or ten hours a week and it was too much. No, said the doctor, the knee-cap, the patella, is misaligned, it's not tracking properly. When my legs straightened out as an adolescent or a boy or whenever it was, my knee got left behind, apparently. It's turned inward. Invasive surgery was not required, said the doctor. I was surprised, a little disappointed. I wanted a new knee. Instead I was sent to see the physio who told me to do the same strength-building exercises suggested by the knee specialist in New Orleans. These simple exercises, she said, would help to pull the knee back into place. And yet, incredibly, after waiting all these years to have my knee sorted out *I am not doing the exercises*. I have waited three years to get my knees repaired, I thought to myself as the train tugged itself into motion once more, and I am not doing the exercises, the simple, strength-building exercises which are necessary to prevent my knee causing me untold and probably intolerable pain in the future. These exercises are intended not just to repair my knee; they are intended to *save* my knee – and I am not doing them. For the first two weeks I turned up with feeble excuses about why I had not done my exercises. Then, on the phone, I made feeble excuses about why I had not turned up to my appointments; then I stopped phoning and made feeble excuses to myself. Instead I stay at home with my knee, my aching knee, asking myself *why* I can't do the exercises. In a fraction of the time spent sitting here thinking about my knee and how much it hurts I could get on with the exercises which would eliminate the pain in my knee, I thought to myself as the train gathered speed, but instead of *doing* the exercises I sit here *thinking* about how I should be doing them. And I shouldn't be thinking about my knee *or* the exercises, of course; I should be getting on with my book about D. H. Lawrence, instead of which I am fretting about my aches and pains. My knee is not the problem, that's for sure: it's a symptom of this larger disease, this inability to carry on with anything, this rheumatism of the will, this chronic inability to see anything through.

That's the big problem but there are lots of minor ones too. Like the way I keep pulling muscles in my lower back. Being tall and weak and narrow-shouldered I am always waiting for my back to 'go', as they say. I avoid lifting things because I am terrified – especially after the moped crash on

Alonissos – of a slipped disc. As for my neck, I don't even wait for that to 'go'. It's *always* about to 'go'. Either it is about to 'go' or it has just 'gone'. Cricked neck: a quaint term for an agonising near-paralysis which, fortunately, only lasts for a day or two and which, unfortunately, only mends for a day or two before it 'goes' again.

I was getting in a terrible state on the train, thinking about all my ailments, but I was also aware that my ailments were taking my mind off the woman with flu who had taken my mind off the fact that the train was running late and would be running even later after the unscheduled pause in the countryside...

Oh, and there's my alopecia: my beard has stopped growing in two patches. This has happened twice before: on each occasion – if the word occasion can embrace periods lasting for a minimum of eighteen months – my beard stopped growing in two 50p-sized patches on either side of my jaw. If I don't shave I look like a mangy dog and so I have to shave every day which makes my sensitive skin come out in a rash. The doctor did not recommend a specialist for alopecia because it is only a cosmetic problem – a cosmetic problem which, of course, has deep-rooted psychological causes and consequences (I can never grow a Lawrentian beard to hide behind). Alopecia is a nervous affliction, apparently, a sign of inner malaise. The best cure is not to think about it but one of the symptoms of alopecia is that you think about it every time you look in a mirror. Every time you think 'I wonder if my alopecia is getting better' you postpone your recovery by a month. Since I wonder about my alopecia between ten and twenty times a day I would need to live to over two hundred in order to stand a chance of recovery from my current bout of alopecia.

The prognosis for my nose had been much better. Shortly after I went to the doctor about my knees and just before I sought his advice about my alopecia I was there asking about another much-needed repair. I'd been getting nose-bleeds for over twenty years, I explained, ever since I was hit in the face during that fight with Paul Hynes in the school playground, but in recent years it had been bleeding more. Having arranged for me to see the knee specialist, the doctor arranged for me to see the nose specialist. It was all part of my project to repair the ravages of what I like to think of as the wandering years, the savage pilgrimage whose Mecca has turned out to be Dullford, England. The nose specialist examined the tubes behind my nose by peering into them with a very thin telescope that made my eyes water. Everything was okay, he said, to my great relief; all he needed to do was cauterise the nose. Fine, I said. If it was okay by me, the doctor said, a student doctor would do the actual cauterising. Fine, I said. When the student doctor had finished jabbing around the regular doctor had a bash too. Oh well, I thought as I walked home, a wad of Kleenex pressed to my numbly traumatised nose, at least I won't have to worry about my nose bleeding every couple of days. No, now it bleeds every couple of hours. If my experience is anything to go by having your nose cauterised to stop it bleeding means that your nose will bleed all the time. It will bleed more often and it will bleed more heavily, for longer periods of time. What to do? Go back and get it re-cauterised? Then what? Then it will bleed ten or twenty times a day; perhaps it will never not be bleeding.

Still, I thought to myself as the train pulled into Dullford, thank heaven for small mercies: that's another of my mottoes these days. At least there's nothing wrong with the heart, the chest, the lungs. Not like Lawrence who was ill right in the centre of the body, in the core of his being. 'Don't for heaven's sake get into the way of being ill!' he wrote. 'That's what I've done – and heaven, I'd give anything to be well.'

No prizes for guessing why I haven't written anything for the last week. I've been in bed with flu. A new, virulent strain of flu that came on while I was in Denmark where I was supposed to give a lecture on Lawrence and Englishness, a subject I had wanted to address for a long time. I hadn't written out a fully prepared text before leaving, just a few notes to get me going. After that I could improvise. Besides, I had a day and a half free and so I had plenty of time to prepare my talk while I was in Denmark. When not preparing my talk on Lawrence – which was all the time because I did not prepare my talk – I did the only thing you can do in these cold places; I stayed in my hotel and watched telly. Except there was no telly to speak of so I had to go out drinking, out into the cold and back into the warm. That's all you do in Denmark. You endure the cold and you drink. You go outside into the cold and back inside to the warm. Outside it's freezing, inside it's boiling. Coats on, coats off. Freezing, boiling. A recipe for flu. The morning before I was due to present my paper my throat started hurting; by lunchtime I was swallowing balls of hot swarf. By mid-afternoon I had a splitting headache. People often say they have splitting headaches and by this they usually mean they have a slight headache but I had a splitting headache in the sense that my head felt like a log being split by an axe, a knot-infested log that is difficult to split and requires constant bashing. To make matters worse, as the time for my talk approached, I began to get nervous because I knew I had not prepared my talk properly. I had not prepared it properly because it is better to improvise, better to talk without notes if you can talk without notes. The problem for me is that I can't talk without notes, I am a hopeless speaker and each time I give a talk I resolve that next time I will prepare the text of my lecture perfectly, word for word. But I never do prepare my talks because it is better to improvise and it is only minutes before the talk that I realise I have nothing to say and so I frantically try to organise my talk and realise that it is too late. It is always like this but it was worse in Denmark because in addition to having nothing to say I was also going down with what was clearly a virulent strain of flu, i.e. a very bad cold.

I arrived at the sparsely populated lecture hall and was introduced as someone 'who has been researching a biography of D. H. Lawrence'. I stood up, explained that I had just gone down with a virulent strain of flu, that I was not quite myself today. I blew my nose, took a gulp of water.

'D. H. Lawrence,' I began, 'David Herbert Lawrence, the same Bert Lawrence who claimed he had never been "our Bert", was an English writer. A simple statement. But let's think about the two parts of this, uh, statement. Do we mean he was a writer who was English? Or that he was an Englishman who wrote? Or both? And even when we concentrate on just one of these two terms we discover that that too is made up of two parts: English and man,' I said, relieved to have scrambled through this thicket of 'thats' and 'twos'. I vaguely remembered a quote by Lawrence, something about being an Englishman, yes, but he was a man before he was an

Englishman. In scurrying through my memory like this I lost my drift somewhat. 'So, um, we have three terms: English, Writer, and Man.' I looked up: people were taking *notes*. I blew my nose again. My nose started bleeding. I dabbed at it with a Kleenex, sniffed back the blood which began trickling down my throat. 'I want to look at the way that these three terms help define and illuminate and elucidate each other. I want to look at each of them in turn and then look at how they coalesce, come together, are embodied in fact in one English man who was a writer, in this case D. H. Lawrence...'

And so it went on. That was pretty much the sum total of my talk on Lawrence and Englishness. Making a big show of how bad I was feeling – much wiping of nose, sipping of water – I shuttled back and forth between these three words, constructing something that was utterly devoid of substance, totally meaningless, in fact, intent only on getting to the forty-five-minute mark and swallowing back the blood from my nose. My head pounded, my voice grated, and through all this flu-induced discomfort throbbed the even worse pain of unqualified humiliation and disgrace. 'And so, to sum up,' I concluded, 'we can see that not only is this simple statement that Lawrence was an English writer problematic but that each of the two terms – the two terms that actually turn out, on closer examination to be three terms – are in turn problematic. But it is only out of this matrix of ambiguity, contradiction and... and so forth that the problems inherent in each of these three terms is resolved – resolved in the figure of the English writer-man, D. H. Lawrence. Thank you.'

I wiped my nose and sat down. I couldn't bring myself to

look at the audience or my host, the distinguished professor who had invited me here. I was aware of a silence, stunned at first but with a smirk around the edges. The distinguished professor thanked me for my 'provocative' talk and then asked if there were any questions. I coughed some blood from my throat into a wad of Kleenex, hoping by this Lawrentian touch to persuade my audience of the all-consuming bond that existed between the speaker and the subject of his talk. No one noticed and no questions were forthcoming. The distinguished professor thanked me for coming all this way to give a talk, especially since I was evidently not in the best of health. There were titters from the audience and the first patter of faint applause. Going full out for the sympathy vote now, I coughed more blood theatrically into my Kleenex – too much: some of it, semi-congealed, spilled over the tissue on to my hand and shirt. Through the polite applause I heard a groan of disgust. I was devastated. I declined the invitation to dinner on the grounds that I was feeling too ill but really because I was too mortified by my own performance to face anyone. I had never felt worse in my life.

The next morning I felt even worse. Initially because of the shame of the previous day's 'lecture', later because, as the plane descended, I found I couldn't equalise my right ear. In addition to my still-splitting headache and my swarf throat I also felt like my right ear was going to explode. Strictly speaking the plane wasn't descending, it was banking and turning in a holding pattern over Heathrow. I asked the flight attendant for a boiled sweet but my ear wouldn't budge. The pain in my ear was so intense that it eased the pain in my head. 'My poor ear,' I kept saying to myself, swallowing and yawning, sucking a sliver of boiled sweet. I'd had an abscess in the same ear when I was a boy. I lay in my mother's arms, apparently, my ear full of that inexplicable pain of childhood, saying 'Press, Mummy, press.' My ear kept popping and my mum kept pressing, I thought to myself as we banked and turned over Heathrow, pressing my ear, swallowing and yawning, trying to unblock my ear. Often in planes I find myself thinking of having sex with the flight attendant: pushing my hand up between her legs as she walks past, fucking in the toilet: standard in-flight porno stuff; now I thought of lying in a flight attendant's arms saying 'Press, Mummy, press.' I was a sickly child. I was off school for so long that the truant officer came round to see what was happening. As well as my terrible eczema I had terrible warts, about fifty of them on my fingers. One day a boy at school told me that they were really good warts, they looked just like real ones. An early example of what I later learned is termed irony. The warts were burned off with dry ice – solidified carbon dioxide? – one day in Gloucester. They turned purple and then vanished. As compensation my parents bought me an outfit for my Action Man: Snow Patrol with white camouflage outfit, skis and green goggles. A strange choice – it was June – but we spent the rest of the afternoon in the garden at home, in the sun. My father took the day off work, or maybe that was another day, when I had some teeth out. After I had the teeth out I spat blood on to the pavement as we walked to the shop to buy an Action Man outfit. My mother said I should use a handkerchief and spit into that – as I had tried to do in the lecture hall in Denmark – instead of on to the pavement. It is possible that the Action Man Snow Patrol outfit was bought as compensation for the teeth not the warts.

I remembered all these things when I was back in

England, enduring the flu, and recovering from the ill-fated lecture in Denmark. Writers suffer more from the flu than other people and I suffer more from the flu than other writers. If you're going out to an office or a factory every day then there's always a holiday element in being sick. You might not feel great but you are at least having a few days at home: it's a rest, a chance to watch afternoon telly. Whereas writers are home all day anyway; they can watch all the afternoon telly they want. What the flu does is stop them working – so there *is*, albeit in heavily diluted form, a sense of being on some kind of holiday. Whereas for me, even when I was feeling a hundred per cent I rarely got down to any work. I could be in the best of health and all I did was mope around, shuffle around in my slippers, wait for the early-evening news. In terms of what I got up to on a daily basis there was next to no difference between my healthy routine and my flu routine. Basically, I realised when I was laid up with flu, I lived each day as though I was laid up with flu even when I didn't have flu. Having flu made no difference – except that I felt terrible. As well as feeling terrible from flu I also felt terrible about the way that I squandered my flu-less days – and by squandering my flu-less days I also made the days when I had flu even worse because if I had stuck to a rigid work schedule I could at least have enjoyed flu as a relief from work. As it was, having flu was simply an intensification of everyday misery; all flu did, I realised, was render bearable misery unbearable. But in retrospect even this unbearable misery – I've said it before and I might well say it again – turns out to have been bearable. Life is bearable even when it's unbearable: that is what is so terrible, that is the unbearable thing about it.

*

Just as I was getting over the last stages of flu, my agent called to say that one of Lawrence's plays was being performed, *The Widowing of Mrs Holroyd*. Did I want to go?

'When is it?' I said.

'Thursday night.'

'Oh, Thursday I'm going to see Nusrat.'

'Who?'

'Nusrat Fateh Ali Khan, the qawali singer. That's a shame. I would like to have come,' I said, thinking how fortunate it was that they overlapped. I had not been to the theatre for twenty years and I had no intention of going again now. It was not even a question of liking or disliking the theatre. The important thing was the pleasure that came from not being interested in the theatre. I am interested in all sorts of things but it is lovely to not be interested in the theatre. Not being interested in the theatre means a whole area of life and culture means nothing to me: there are entire sections of listings magazines that I don't need to consult, vast areas of conversation I don't need to take part in, great wads of cash that I don't need to consider parting with. It is bliss, not being interested in the theatre. Not being interested in the theatre provides me with more happiness than all the things I am interested in put together. There is a moral here. To be interested in something is to be involved in what is essentially a stressful relationship with that thing, to suffer anxiety on its behalf.

Take Nusrat who I was going to see on the same night I had been invited to *The Widowing of Mrs Holroyd*. He had played twice at the Théâtre de la Ville when I lived in Paris and both times I wanted to see him even though this was next to impossible because everything at the Théâtre de la

Ville is sold out months in advance. Both times I called the box office but the phones were always engaged. Both times I turned up at the Théâtre de la Ville in person to have it confirmed that the concerts were sold out. Both times I turned up at the Théâtre de la Ville well before the concerts were due to begin with a little home-made sign reading '*Je cherche une place*', both times I took my place among the dozens of other Nusrat fans who didn't have tickets and were holding signs saying '*Je cherche une place*'. The first time, right up until the concert began, I was hoping that I would be lucky but I was not. I went home, far unhappier, far more disappointed than if I had not turned up with my little home-made sign. The second time I turned up even earlier and did manage to buy a ticket, from a scalper, for twice the official price. I had an hour and a half to kill before the concert and I sat in the Sarah Bernhardt Café thinking about the way I had paid twice the asking price to get into this gig. Once inside I realised I had one of the three or four worst seats in the house, and I spent the first half of the concert thinking how much more I would have enjoyed it from a better vantage point. The second half I spent worrying that this particular concert of Nusrat's was not nearly as good as the concerts by him that I had already attended. Then, when I got out, all I could think of was the way that, had I not been so preoccupied by the price and location of the seat, I might well have enjoyed this concert as much as the previous ones. Uppermost in my mind, though, was the question that was sure to be uppermost in my mind when I went to see him again on Thursday: why did I keep making such efforts to see Nusrat when I had already seen him play ten or twelve times previously?

Compare that with the bliss of not being interested in

theatre, of knowing nothing about it, of never being tempted to go! Oh bliss of indifference!

So there was no question of going to see *The Widowing of Mrs Holroyd* but the fact remained that though this was a play it was also a play by D. H. Lawrence who I am very interested in, in whom I now have what might be termed a vested interest. Lawrence, in other words, as is the case with all things in which I am interested, is primarily a source of stress and anxiety, is even intruding on that lovely lacuna of disinterest and indifference, the theatre.

But that, of course, is why I was interested in writing a book about Lawrence: to enable me to pass into the realm of complete disinterest. Lawrence said that one sheds one's sickness in books; I would say that one sheds one's interest. Once I have finished this book on Lawrence, depend upon it, I will have no interest in him whatsoever. One begins writing a book about something because one is interested in that subject; one finishes writing a book in order to lose interest in that subject: the book itself is a record of this transition.

If I didn't write this book I would probably go on being interested in Lawrence for the rest of my days. He would gnaw away at me. I would always be curious about *Women in Love*, would always be thinking to myself, 'Ah maybe today I will re-read *Women in Love*', would always be looking out for new books about Lawrence, would always be making notes about Lawrence or thinking that I might one day write a book about him, whereas once I have finished this book – if I can force myself to retain interest in Lawrence for long enough to complete it – Lawrence will become a closed book for me. That's what I look forward to: no longer having anything to do with Lawrence.

When nothing interests you any longer, I think to myself, looking at the place on the shelves which will one day be occupied by my book which is intermittently about Lawrence, then you can stop writing and be happy: then you can despair.

First, though, I had to go to Taos to try to make up for that earlier, post-Oaxaca failure to get there.

In 1926, unable to face the exertion of the journey from Europe, Lawrence had declared that 'it would be marvellous if one could just fly over to New Mexico'; seventy years on, we did exactly that. Or inexactly that: we flew to San Francisco where I would love to live, where Laura grew up, and where, within days of arriving, we vowed we *would* live, one day. Laura was especially pleased to be back in California: it gave her a chance to practise her Spanish.

We were not sure how to get from San Francisco to Taos, whether to hire a car in San Francisco and drive all the way to Taos and back, or to fly to Las Vegas and then hire a car. It was a difficult decision. In principle we should have driven: that way we would be travellers like Lawrence and Frieda, real people passing through real places; if we flew we would be passengers, suspended in the non-place of the pressurised cabin. Besides, I liked driving in America, was looking forward to driving. The problem was that Laura couldn't drive and though I was looking forward to doing lots of driving I was also worried about doing too much driving and thereby changing the pleasure of driving into the chore of driving so that by the time we got to Taos it was quite possible that I would be heartily sick of driving. We had heard of absurdly cheap tickets to Vegas, fares designed to lure punters to the casinos, but when we called the airlines these fares were not available. We had heard of 'companion fares' to Vegas but these also were unavailable. All available fares to Vegas were unavailable. That should have settled it: the fact that it was not practical to fly to Vegas should have meant that we drove to Taos but because arranging flights was proving so awkward I became determined to fly. We eventually made reservations for Albuquerque but then, having worried that the drive from San Francisco was too long, I became worried that I wouldn't do *enough* driving and so we decided, finally, to fly to Salt Lake City – a place neither of us had any desire to go – and take a circuitous, logic-free drive to Taos.

As we flew over Nevada, a cloud printed an ink-blot shadow, exactly the shape of the British Isles, on the arid nothingness below.

Unused to driving and unsure about the handling of our rental car, I was, as Laura wrote in her account of her trip – her 'memoirs' as she liked to refer to them – *'nervous'* as we struggled to navigate our way out of the airport. 'Nervous', in this context, meant uptight, prone to erupt in anger at the slightest difficulty – and there were many difficulties since Laura, for all her linguistic skills, has no sense of direction and is, consequently, a very poor navigator. '*After much quarrelling*,' she wrote later, '*we managed to find our way out of Salt Lake City and drive south-west through Utah*' – 'south-west', in this context, meaning 'south-east'.

We spent the night in Moab where, having ended one day with an unappetising dinner, we began the next with a foul breakfast. Of the two of us, I am not sure who came out worse: even though I don't like eggs, I ordered eggs and got eggs; Laura ordered fresh fruit and was served canned peaches. Still, we were up early, the sky was perfect – three snow-streak clouds over the horizon – and, after much scanning, we had found a classic rock station on FM. It was a sealed experience: driving along the highway, listening to songs on the radio about roaring along the highway, listening to the radio.

By lunchtime we were driving through the massive undisappointment of Monument Valley.

'Cinema,' I said.

'CinemaScope,' corrected Laura.

Across the border, in Arizona, we joined the perpetual rush-hour of tour buses, R.V.s, cars and campers crawling nose-to-tail through the Grand Canyon. We stayed just long enough to satisfy the need *to have seen* the Grand Canyon, to be able to *say* that we had seen the Grand Canyon – which I had seen before – and pressed on to Flagstaff. It was a relief to be back in the tranquillity of a city after the clamour and near gridlock of the Canyon but we were once again faced with a wretched dinner – 'G. *had a fit, as usual*' – that I found difficult to stomach.

The next day we were up even earlier than usual, heading east through the Painted Desert and the Petrified Forest. We stopped there, at a spot called Agate Bridge, just as I had done six years previously in the middle of a long drive across America, and stood in the place I had stood before. At the time it had been a major detour, driving through Arizona, but I had decided it was worthwhile because there was so little chance of ever finding myself in this part of the world again. If I was ever going to drive through the Painted Desert, I had reasoned, this was the time to do it. And now, six years later, I had driven through the Painted Desert again, had come to the same spot I had been in six years previously – and I had done so *precisely because I had stood here before*. Strange, the pleasure derived from revisiting a place. It has nothing to do with getting to know an area better or more thoroughly; all that counts is the simple physical fact of having been in the same spot before. I have stood here before, I thought to myself as I stood there surrounded by the same stripes of colour, the same silence, am once again filling the space that has remained empty throughout the long years of my absence. It was as if a meeting had taken place, a rendezvous. In Taormina, outside the Fontana Vecchia, I had tried to enhance my responsiveness to the place by reminding myself that I was standing where Lawrence had stood, was seeing the things he had seen. It hadn't worked. But here, in the Painted Desert, I was moved by the fact that I was standing in the place *I* had stood, was seeing the things *I* had seen. They were of no consequence, these thoughts, but I thought them. And if, at that moment, I had been asked who I was I would have replied unhesitatingly: I am the person who stood here six years ago. What I didn't wonder, as I stood there again, was if I would ever stand here again. Each time we leave places like this, in remote parts of the world, we do so for the last time.

'We both got fierce headaches from the relentless wind,' wrote Laura, 'but the Painted Desert was one of the highlights of our frenzied trip.'

We spent the night in Gallup, a strip of motel signs telephoto'd alongside the railroad tracks. Laura was happy to be in New Mexico ('*The licence plates here are much nicer than the ones in Arizona.*') and even happier to be on Route 66 – if we *were* on it. Difficult to say for sure, difficult to know what, if anything, remained of that stretch of post-fabricated, vinyl-macadamed mythology. '*There were dozens of motels with lovely names like Cactus Motel or Desert Sands or Desert Skies but we ended up checking into one with a very ordinary name: the Days Inn.*' It was a Sunday night and, as far as we could make out, there was only one restaurant open. '*G. had a breakdown because he couldn't find anything that suited him on the menu. He asked the waitress to point out the vegetarian dishes about ten times, each time deciding that it was all too disgusting, and finally lost it. What an idiot!*'

After that we needed a drink but, according to New Mexico law, all bars are closed on Sundays. We couldn't even buy beer to drink in our room at the motel where the vertical hold on the TV left much to be desired. The only thing to do was have sex but Laura didn't want to. I didn't want to either: it was only the fact that Laura didn't want to that made me want to. In the end we just lay on the bed, watching the TV flip round like fruit on a slot machine, listening to the shunting, the iron-rumble of the Santa Fe freights.

The next morning I once again '*fell prey to a terrible attack after a fearful blueberry pancake covered in sour cream that had gone sour. Off we stormed!*' Ah, we may have stormed, Laura, but at least, by now, we were storming in the right direction. After a meandering start, Laura had got into navigating in a big way. We exited Gallup without a single U-turn and headed, like an arrow, towards Santa Fe. As we drove we supplemented our normal competition – who would be first to identify the band, track and the album from which it was taken, on the classic rock station we were tuned to? – with another: who could name the most Indian tribes?

'I'll go first,' said Laura, shouting to make herself heard above Tonto's Expanding Headband. 'Sioux.'

'Navajo.'

'Apache.'

'Comanche.'

'Mohican.'

After that it became difficult. 'Pawnee,' I said, after a pause.

'Shoshone.'

'Cherokee.'

'Comanche,' said Laura,

'I've already said "Comanche",' I said, but before I could gloat over my victory we saw a body hanging from a ranch entrance sign, swaying in the wind. We backed up and saw that it was actually a guy, stuffed and dressed in hat, shirt, jeans and boots. Even close-up, silhouetted by the sun, it seemed like a real body hanging by the neck. Written on the gallows ranch-sign were the words 'We Do Things The Old Way: Keep Out'. It was the lack of spelling mistakes that convinced us that the warning was a joke: in this part of the world a message of genuinely ill intent, however simple, would always be enhanced by a missed 'h' or a dropped vowel.

In Santa Fe the word 'adobe' was on our lips and in our eyes constantly. We couldn't move for adobe buildings selling adobe pots in which to eat adobe-coloured burritos. We walked around for an hour, looking at the Navajo rugs and turquoise jewellery but by now I was in a frenzy of impatience to get to Taos. Besides, Santa Fe didn't quite live up to the immense romance of the name we had seen on the sides of the freights at Gallup. It had a peculiarly *indoors* quality: beige buildings, magnolia sky. Even the thermometer on the street showed 68 degrees: room temperature. Laura was keen on looking for turquoise ear-rings and Navajo rugs but I insisted on the importance of getting to Taos 'in good time' even though there was nothing to hurry to Taos for.

Once we got in the car, though, I hurried to Taos as if there were no today let alone tomorrow. Laura, who had now assumed overall responsibility for all matters pertaining to route and maps, insisted on our taking scenic Highway 63, the so-called 'turquoise trail', but we didn't get much opportunity to admire the scenery. Having lost control of our route I concentrated on determining our pace. I floored the accelerator whenever the road was clear, passed every car in sight, took curves at speeds that reminded us of the crash at Alonissos. It was the fault, primarily, of the classic rock station which kept drumming up support for the pleasures of flat-out rhythmic velocity.

It was late afternoon by the time we checked into La Fonda, the hotel where Lawrence's paintings are kept. There was no sign of the owner, Saki Karavas, but Johnny, the receptionist, was there to welcome us. He smoked with one hand while, with the other, he fixed some kind of clear tube into his nose. He had the driest skin ever seen on a human being. Magnified a few million times it could have passed for a close-up of a log in the Petrified Forest. We were booked into the Tyrone Power and Somebody Else Honeymoon suite, he said. I asked after Saki who, according to Johnny, was around some place but was not feeling himself today. I took this to mean – as I had ever since the debacle in Denmark when I had excused myself in identical terms – that Saki was utterly himself today: there comes a point in our lives when we are most often and most emphatically ourselves on those days when we like to think we are not ourselves.

Perched on the dresser in our room, black and guilty, omens – for all I knew – of theft, illness or death, were two birds. They lunged over the bed as we entered, flung themselves out of the window, leaving a flurry of wings in their wake. They scared us. From the window we watched them fly low over the adobe plaza and take their place on a telegraph pole. They could easily have been a thousand years old or more, those birds. Like us they watched the humans coming in and out of gift shops, parking their pick-ups at meters. An Indian in a cowboy hat walked by. The birds flew off.

I wanted to head out to the Lawrence ranch but Laura said we should save that for the next day as it would soon be dark. Instead we drove up to the pueblo where two hundred Indians still live without water or electricity. A police car was waiting in the middle of the road, facing us. I pulled alongside and wound down the window. The policeman, an Indian, said that the pueblo was closed for religious ceremonies and would not be open to the public again until Monday. We couldn't hang around till Monday. Therefore we would not see the pueblo: a blow that was also a relief. If the pueblo had been open I would have visited it and set down my impressions, would have tried to sense if the 'old nodality' Lawrence spoke of still held good. As it was, there was nothing we could do. It was not our fault that the pueblo was closed – as it often was, apparently. Keeping visitors out was a way of retaining that old nodality and we had played our part in perpetuating it.

Laura was keen to see a ghost town mentioned in one of the guide books and so we headed out past Eagle Nest in search of Elizabethtown. We drove as far as Red River, a town that had the look of a ghost town in the process of formation. By that time we were miles beyond the expected location of Elizabethtown. We had missed it completely: it had become the ghost of a ghost town, had lost even the phantom of nodality. Anywhere we went that afternoon, it seemed, was going to be either closed or non-existent. We decided to return to Taos and kick back for the rest of the day.

Both the Moby Dickens Bookstore and the Taos Bookstore had selections of out-of-print, Lawrence-related titles but there was no sign of *Phoenix*. Laura was browsing through the shops selling Navajo jewellery and rugs. I was already sick of the sight of gift shops selling Navajo jewellery and rugs and so I bought her a turquoise necklace. That seemed to do the trick but, in addition to the gift shops, there were the galleries to contend with. They were also gift shops really. I had thought there were a lot of bad artists in Santa Fe but it could not begin to compete with Taos in that respect. Taos had an unrivalled concentration of terrible artists. There were more terrible artists living in Taos than anywhere else on earth. That was where its nodality lay.

Speaking of painters who could not paint, Johnny, at the '*freaky*' hotel, offered to show us Lawrence's pictures. The plastic tube to Johnny's nose, we saw now, was about twenty feet long and was connected to a beer-barrel of liquid oxygen. Like an astronaut he trailed this umbilical supply of oxygen into Saki's image-crammed study. There were dozens of photos of Saki with various celebrities (all signed), and many pictures of Brett and Frieda. Lawrence's paintings jostled for wall-space along with all the other images. They were far, far worse than reproductions lead one to expect. Ridiculous really, full of leery smiles and lascivious cavorting, but it must have been fun, I suppose, to have painted all that flesh. At various times Saki had offered to ship the paintings back to England in exchange for the Elgin Marbles being returned to Greece but no one in England was interested. In a way it was appropriate that the paintings remain here; they set the low standard that all Taos-based artists sought to emulate.

We ate dinner in a deserted Mexican place with lovely pink walls and blue chairs. It was like eating in a large doll's house. Pink and blue mariachi music played on a stereo. Laura spoke with the waiter who spoke almost no English. The only other customer was a woman with a baby.

'*Es un niño o una niña?*' said Laura, holding the baby's little finger.

'Excuse me?'

'I'm sorry. Is it a he or a she?'

'A she,' said the mother.

'What's her name?'

'Sierra,' said the mother, a painter, as it happened.

'*Tiene un niño?*' the waiter asked Laura.

'*Estoy gastando toda mi energía en cuidarme del niño,*' she said, pointing at me.

The food was good but by now we were fed up with eating in restaurants. We'd had our fill of finding places to eat, ordering, waiting, eating, asking for the check, calculating the tip and paying. We had reached that state often observed in couples on holiday: left to ourselves we were beyond conversation. Every five minutes I said, 'I'm exhausted' and Laura said, 'Me too.' Then we lapsed into silence until, after five minutes, Laura said, 'I'm so tired.'

'Me too,' I said.

After dinner we went to the Taos Inn for drinks where Laura updated her memoirs. Sandwiched between details of our trip she composed a blood-boltered history of the region, stunning in its brevity:

> *Spanish settlers and soldiers accompanied by priests reached New Mexico in 1598. But in 1680, the Indians revolted and killed many Spanish settlers. Then came the invading Comanches, who terrorised everyone. American Indians won US citizenship & the right to vote in 1924.*

While Laura was finishing her memoirs I got talking to Gary, a checked-shirt-wearer in his fifties whose hair was less grey than mine. He had grown up a Catholic in an Italian-American family. Later he married and had five children. Then, in his mid-forties, he had come out of the closet, become a militant gay activist, and moved into the Castro in San Francisco. That, he said, was when he found himself. Next he converted to Judaism and moved to Taos with his lover, Steve. He could have converted to anything and everything as far as I was concerned, but he would always be a Catholic at heart: why else this need to confess to a total stranger? Partly because I am a good listener. People are always telling me their life stories and they always tell me they have done so because I am a good listener. In fact I am a terrible listener, I don't listen to a word: what I am doing is *looking* like I am listening while concentrating all my energy on not listening, on finding some refuge beyond what is being said. It is easy to be a good listener in America: all you have to do is not interrupt and it is easy not to interrupt when you are not paying attention. Still, I had listened to this guy enough to be irritated by his story, by the way finding himself meant losing himself in widening circles of group identification. I liked Lawrence's angry insistence – 'I am no more than a single human man wandering my lonely way across these years' – on being oneself, not a gay man, or a Jew or an Englishman.

Gary's lover, Steve, showed up and in that friendly American way we got talking to a large group of people. Laura was speaking Spanish while I listened, in English, to Steve telling me about Taos.

'I feel so at home here,' he said, 'something special. You know what I mean?'

'A kind of nodality?' I said.

'You know, do you believe in reincarnation, Jim?' He had got the idea, as Americans sometimes do, that my name was Jim.

'Well . . .' I said.

'Uh-huh. Well you know I have such feeling for this place, had such a feeling for this place the first time I came here. The first time I came here it was like I had been here before. A psychic said I was a Navajo Indian in a previous life.'

'Well Steve,' I said reasonably. 'If there *is* such a thing as reincarnation, you can be pretty sure that the life you had before was even more boring than this one. For every half-decent life you get you probably have to have a hundred dull ones. The chances are that in your previous life you were a clerk at the IRS or a waiter in a diner at Gallup. If your previous life had anything to do with Taos and the Indians you were probably selling Navajo jewellery in a gift shop.' Steve took no offence. You can say what you like to a certain kind of American and as long as you don't say it aggressively or use abusive language it is all the same to them. Just to be on the safe side, though, I bought him a bottle of Anchor Steam. By the time he bought me one my earlier irritation had all but vanished. I was enjoying sitting round the campfire like this, pow-wowing with people I may have known in previous lives – may even have *been* in previous lives – but whom I had only just got round to meeting in this one.

'Actually Steve, do you know what I really believe I was in a previous life?' I said later. I had built up a full head of Anchor Steam and was feeling the sudden surge of borrowed illumination. 'I believe that I was exactly the same as I am now, in this one. That I lived this life before, in every detail, that everything that happened to me and will happen to me has happened before and will happen again, including this conversation. Now and throughout all eternity.'

'That's a scary concept, Jim,' said Steve.

'Don't worry, he's not himself today,' said Laura. 'Come on Lorenzo. Let's go to bed.' She had taken to calling me Lorenzo – I liked it – in honour of our arrival in Taos.

Back at the *'loony'* hotel, slumped in a chair, evidently not himself, Saki was waiting for us. He looked like he had minutes left to live. Compared with his boss, Johnny had discovered the secret of eternal middle age. He had traded in his earlier oxygen supply and now had a smaller, portable one on his back, so that he looked less like an astronaut than a scuba diver, albeit one in permanent recovery from a severe bout of the bends. Possessed of a kind of somnolent determination Saki insisted on taking us into his office and showing us the paintings Johnny had shown us earlier in the day. He pointed at the walls and we went through the whole routine Johnny had taken us through a few hours earlier. I believed in the eternal recurrence but I didn't think things recurred so rapidly. Laura plied Saki with questions and exclaimed with pleased surprise every time he reached into his filing cabinets and pulled out a magazine article about himself and Lawrence's banned paintings. There were magazines in every language, especially Japanese, and they all featured pictures of Saki in his study surrounded by Lawrence's paintings. Magazine after magazine, all showing pictures of himself in the room in which I was now standing, looking at magazines.

Laura was sleepy in the morning.

'I had funny dreams,' she said, lying in the crook of my arm. 'I kept dreaming of maps and turn-offs.'

'I dreamt that I was back in that office, looking at the Lawrence paintings again,' I said. 'Then I realised it wasn't a dream. I *was* in there again.' More exactly I was watching a video of the room: just as I was leaving Saki's office and heading for bed he had persuaded me to watch a cassette of a film that had been made about the paintings in his office. To minimise the chances of getting shown around Lawrence's paintings again, we got up, checked out of La Fonda and set off for the Lawrence Ranch.

To the west was a great expanse of mesa and, in the blue distance, a line of mountains. To the east, sloping hills. It was windy. Clouds were stampeding across the sky. The wind bumped the car, urging it off the road. Fifteen minutes out of Taos we turned off the highway on to a gravel road. Trees were springing into bud. The vastness was behind us, in the rear-view; ahead there was the shrinking that always accompanies approach.

We stopped the car and stepped out into the wind. Compared with the places we had driven through this particular setting seemed sheltered rather than engulfed by the spaciousness celebrated by Lawrence. The emptiness lay far off, in the distance. A path led to Frieda's grave. Behind it was the shrine built by Angelo Ravagli, where Lawrence's ashes were buried. A nice spot. The size of a white bus shelter, the shrine had a steeply angled roof with Lawrence's symbol, a phoenix, carved at the apex. It was easy to imagine the scene described by Auden when he came here in 1939: 'Cars of women pilgrims go up every day to stand reverently there and wonder what it would have been like to sleep with him.'

At the back of the shrine was an altar of sorts, emblazoned with another phoenix and inscribed with the initials D.H.L. that had been printed on that other object of worship, the travelling trunk in Eastwood. There were few comments in the visitors book, mainly just names and addresses. The day before, however, someone had wondered 'what D.H.L. and Frieda would think of today's gender warfare. One thing I'm sure of: the macho male drivers on our highways – the ones with feet stuck to the accelerator – would have dismayed him.'

The altar itself was sprinkled with mementoes left by pilgrims: coins (Lawrence would have liked that), a credit card receipt from a store in Brooklyn, half a cinema ticket, a candle, a book of matches, a boiled sweet, an origami frog. A Boston-based attorney, John J. Pentz III, had left his business card. Several people had written personal messages on little scraps of paper. On a large piece of thick paper – from an artist's sketchbook, I think – a poem had been written in bold black ink: 'Words from the Eyes of the Half-Born'. I didn't read it all the way through.

'What do you think of it, Lorenzo?' said Laura.

'I don't know,' I said. 'What about you?'

'It reminds me a little of Jim Morrison's grave in Père-Lachaise,' she said.

Lined by pines, the path back to the ranch led our eyes over the mesa, towards the endless horizon. The wind in the trees was as loud as traffic on the freeway. Laura took a photograph, framing it so that I was standing towards the edge of the vast horizontal landscape. Clouds streamed across the sky.

A note on the door of what we took to be the ranch explained that this building was built after Lawrence had left: the house he and Frieda had lived in was the one immediately behind. We walked around there but were deterred by a vicious dog, enclosed by a wire fence deliberately designed to appear inadequate, to offer the possibility of escape. He kept appearing at different, vulnerable parts of his prison, barking, drooling. Laura said that if you held up a stone and made as if to throw it, that was enough to frighten even the fiercest dog. I picked up a rock, gestured aggressively, and the dog slunk off. A shame really: it was such a nasty dog I would like to have thrown the rock and bloodied its snout, clubbed it to death even.

Lawrence's ranch looked in pretty bad shape. The word 'ranch' had made me think of something along the lines of the Ponderosa but this seemed more house than ranch, more hut than house. The roof was covered in a substance I recognised but whose name I didn't know: a cross between tarpaulin and emery paper. It sagged somewhat, as if it was not quite itself. I thought about Lawrence and all the work, all the DIY, he had done on the house. Out of the sun it was chilly, even in mid-April, and I wondered how cold it must have been in winter, how cosy it must have looked with snow on the hills and in the trees, wood smoke drifting from the chimney.

There was a rocking chair on the porch, decorated with Indian motifs. It had a sad, waiting look that gave it the quality of a loyal dog. Nearby, propped by the door was a broom. Whether or not they had been there in Lawrence's day – almost certainly not – that chair and broom were more expressive of his spirit than any other relics we had seen: they were things that could still be used, that existed for a purpose beyond the simple fact of their preservation.

Laura sat in the rocking chair and began rocking. The sun lurched out from behind a cloud, warming us instantly. Laura rocked back in the chair, angling her face towards the sun and wrinkling her nose in that lovely way she has. I picked up the broom and began sweeping dust from the porch. The wind had dropped. It was sunny and perfectly still. Even the trees were silent. The only sound was the noise of the chair creaking on the wooden porch, the slight rustle of the broom.

Back in San Francisco, at the Green Apple bookstore, I found a copy of *Phoenix*: the Penguin edition. I saw it and snatched it up in the way that one does in these circumstances, fearful that at the last moment someone else was going to beat me to it. Ten dollars – and, right next to it, was *Phoenix II*.

I also bought a discounted copy of Elizabeth Bishop's poetry so that I could read 'Questions of Travel', the poem in which she sets out the fundamental uncertainties contemplated, at times, by all travellers.

> Think of the long trip home.
> Should we have stayed at home and thought of here?
> [. . .]
> What childishness is it that while there's a breath of life
> in our bodies, we are determined to rush
> to see the sun the other way around? [. . .]
> But surely it would have been a pity
> not to have seen the trees along this road,
> really exaggerated in their beauty,
> not to have seen them gesturing
> like noble pantomimists, robed in pink.
> – Not to have had to stop for gas and heard
> the sad, two-noted, wooden tune
> of disparate wooden clogs
> carelessly clacking over
> a grease-stained filling-station floor.

At various times Lawrence wondered why he had drifted so far from his inclination to sit tight: 'What is it, makes one want to go away?' 'Why can't one sit still?' 'Why does one create such discomfort for oneself!' In Taormina we had wondered what was the point of going all that way to see the place where he had lived; in Mexico we had decided, effectively, that there was none. In its myriad contingencies, however, Bishop's answer – her series of incidental answers – is close to definitive: had we not gone to Taormina we would not have heard the old man selling oregano in Furci, would not have been able to sprint across the tracks at Cisterna; had we not gone to Taos we would not have seen that road sign, 'Gusty Winds May Exist', would not have seen the origami frog at the Lawrence shrine or any of the other hundreds of things that we had noticed and not noticed on the way there.

Had we not seen and done all these things we would not be the people we are. To put it even more simply, had we not gone to Taos we would not have come to San Francisco and I would not have found the copy of *Phoenix* that I had been looking for all those years. Maybe it can be boiled down still further: had I not decided to write a book about Lawrence I would not have gone to Taos and would not have found that copy of *Phoenix*. Does that mean, in effect, that I had to write this book in order to find my copy of *Phoenix*? Could such a simple quest really have required such a disproportionate investment of effort? That question begs another, even more difficult one: what to do now, now that I have been to Taos, now that I have found that copy of *Phoenix*?

The more I ponder these questions the more I am persuaded that the real subject of this book, the one that writing it was an attempt to evade, is despair.

My greatest urge in life is to do nothing. It's not even an absence of motivation, a lack, for I *do* have a strong urge: to do nothing. To down tools, to stop. Except I know that if I do that I will fall into despair, and I know that it is worth doing anything in one's power to avoid depression because from there, from being depressed, it is only an imperceptible step to despair: the last refuge of the ego.

Once you are depressed there is almost nothing you can do about it. It is useless trying to snap out of it or buck up because it is impossible to see the point of doing anything. Depression is the complete absence of any interest in anything. You cannot think of a single thing to do, or place to go, or book to read. In his periods of 'huge stagnation' Pessoa's Bernando Soares compared his condition to that of 'a prisoner deprived of normal freedom of action in an infinite prison cell'.

The first time I became depressed I didn't even realise it. I knew I wasn't feeling that great, actually felt pretty terrible, depressed in fact, but since I had no prior experience to go on I didn't realise that what I was experiencing was depression. Second time around there was a familiar cast to the greyness. The third time, though, in Rome, in the wake of our abortive trip to beastly Oaxaca, I had enough previous experience to know that I was depressed – but because, on those previous occasions, I *hadn't* realised that I was depressed I couldn't remember – nor did I care – how I'd gotten over it. Maybe that's the nature of the beast. Getting out of depression is like finding a loophole in the law: you use it once and then it is closed up and sealed off so that it can't be done again.

It went on for a couple of months. Laura went to work while I stayed home and did nothing. I read nothing and did nothing. I spent most of the time watching TV which may not sound so extreme but this was mornings and afternoons, it was *Italian* TV and – the clincher – the TV wasn't even turned on. Nothing interested me – and this, in the end, is what saved me. I had no interest in anything, no curiosity. All I felt was: I am depressed, I am depressed. And then, this depression generated its own flicker of recovery. *I became interested in depression.* Since I was in the grip of something fairly extreme – albeit an extreme state characterised, like the contentment of which it is a negative expression, by the absence of any sense of extremity – I thought I'd look at a couple of books: *Darkness Visible* by William Styron and *Black Sun* by Julia Kristeva. (I must have been feeling bad to have read that old trout!) In the latter I read about the overwhelming effect that Holbein's *Dead Christ* had had on Dostoevsky. Kristeva quoted a chunk from *The Idiot* and I thought I'd like to read that passage for myself, outside of quotation marks, as it were. This reactivated a long-dormant interest in the ways that writers have written about paintings: Rilke on Cézanne and Rodin, Lawrence on his own paintings. I became interested in things again. I began to follow things up. I thought I'd like to go to Switzerland to see Holbein's *Dead Christ*. I began to look forward to my *cornetti integrali* whereas for many weeks previously I had plodded to the Farnese and had scarcely cared whether they had any *cornetti integrali* or not. Now – a sure sign of recovery – I once again became irritated when there were no *cornetti integrali* left. I started complaining and moaning. Most important of all I began to regret things: that I had never visited the Rodin Museum in Paris, that we had not made it to New Mexico where most of Lawrence's paintings were on show, that I had wasted these months when I was too depressed to do anything. I was cured.

I was interested in the world again. Before I knew it I was overrun with things that interested me. I was prevented from pursuing some of the things that interested me by other things that interested me more. I began to take pleasure again in the knowledge that there were things, like the theatre, that I had no interest in.

Now that dodge – getting out of depression by becoming interested in depression – only works once. I've got no interest in depression now. There might be more to learn about it but I'm not interested. The only thing that interests me about depression is staying well clear of it. And since the only way to avoid giving into depression and despair is to do something, even something you hate, *anything* in fact, I force myself to keep bashing away at something, anything. Flaubert said it was only thanks to work that he was 'able to stifle the melancholy' he was born with. It is a simple choice: work or succumb to melancholia, depression and despair. Like it or not you have to try to do something with your life, you have to keep plugging away.

Besides, the alternatives to giving in and giving up are never as simple as they seem. Believe me, I know. I've devoted more of my life to thoughts of giving up than anyone else I can think of. Nietzsche wrote that the thought of suicide had got him through many a bad night, and thinking of giving up is probably the one thing that's kept me going. I think about it on a daily basis but always come up against the problem of what to do when I've given up. Give up one thing and you're immediately obliged to do something else. The only way to give up totally is to kill yourself but that one act requires an assertion of will equal to the total amount that would be expanded in the rest of a normal lifetime. Killing yourself is not giving up, it's more like a catastrophic fast-forwarding, but anything other than suicide imposes an array of disagreeable obligations. All very well to stop living as you do – but then what? Then you have to *start* living in some other way. Stop doing one thing and you have to start another: something else, something even less agreeable, something which would no doubt have you harking back to the life you'd abandoned in five minutes flat.

Let's suppose, for example, that I decided – as, I remind you, I am tempted to on a daily if not hourly basis – now that I have my copy of *Phoenix*, to call it a day, to give up, to abandon any attempt not just at earning a living but at *having a life*. From this moment on, let's say, I will no longer be an active participant in my own life. (Ah, what a delicious thought that is, rippling over one like a dream of luxury!) But what then? What would happen next? Within five minutes I'd be thinking about listening to music and would put a CD on the stereo. Five minutes after that I'd be up again because I would have grown fed up with that piece of music and would be scanning the shelves and shelves of CDs, searching in vain for a piece of music that I was not heartily sick of, thinking to myself that if I had more CDs there would surely be *one* that I would like to listen to. Somewhere on earth, I would say to myself, there must be a CD that I am not yet heartily sick of . . . And before I knew it I would be out of the house and on my way to the Megastore, looking for a new CD.

Should anyone flatter us by asking what we are looking for, what we are searching for, then we think immediately, almost instinctively, in vast terms – God, fulfilment, love – but our lives are actually made up of lots of tiny searches for things like a CD we are not sick of, an out-of-print edition of *Phoenix*, a picture of Lawrence that I saw when I was seventeen, another identical pair of suede shoes to the ones I am wearing now, even, I suppose, a *cornetto integrale*, ideally, a place where they serve perfect *cornetti integrali* each day without fail. Add them together and these little things make up an epic quest, more than enough for one lifetime.

Thinking specifically of the search for CDs, let's assume that after deciding to give up, after sitting around listening to CDs and going out to buy a new CD, I found a CD I liked the idea of listening to. Then I would race back home where I would listen contentedly or disappointedly to the CD for some unspecified period of time, either playing it over and over because I liked it (or certain tracks at any rate) or skimming through it quickly and realising it was a mistake. Still, at some point, whether it was a good buy or not, I would not simply grow tired of listening to this new CD but would actually become heartily sick of the idea of listening to CDs and would think to myself that sitting around listening to CDs is a much more enjoyable activity, a much more enjoyable *inactivity*, if it is a relief from something else — anything else. And so, after squandering a day working through this demoralising routine that I have worked through innumerable days before, I would resign myself, would in fact *abandon* myself to not giving up, to picking up my pen and trying once again, if for no other reason than to render listening to my CDs a little less dispiriting, to make some progress with my study of D. H. Lawrence.

And there you have it. One way or another we all have to write our studies of D. H. Lawrence. Even if they will never be published, even if we will never complete them, even if all we are left with after years and years of effort is an unfinished, unfinishable record of how we failed to live up to our own earlier ambitions, still we all have to try to make some progress with our books about D. H. Lawrence. The world over, from Taos to Taormina, from the places we have visited to countries we will never set foot in, the best we can do is to try to make some progress with our studies of D. H. Lawrence.

NOTES

Abbreviations of Principal Editions Used

Letters Vols. 1–7 refers to the Cambridge University Press edition of Lawrence's letters, respectively:

Volume 1: September 1901 – May 1913, edited by James T. Boulton, 1979.

Volume 2: June 1913 – October 1916, edited by George J. Zytaruk and James T. Boulton, 1981.

Volume 3: October 1916 – June 1921, edited by James T. Boulton and Andrew Robertson, 1984.

Volume 4: June 1921 – March 1924, edited by Warren Roberts, James T. Boulton and Elizabeth Mansfield, 1987.

Volume 5: March 1924 – March 1927, edited by James T. Boulton and Lindeth Vasey, 1989.

Volume 6: March 1927 – November 1928, edited by James T. Boulton, Margaret H. Boulton and Gerald M. Lacy, 1991.

Volume 7: November 1928 – February 1930, edited by Keith Sagar and James T. Boulton, 1993.

Thomas Hardy: Study of Thomas Hardy and Other Essays, edited by Bruce Steele, Cambridge University Press, Cambridge, 1985.

Poems: *The Complete Poems*, edited by Vivian De Sola Pinto and F. Warren Roberts, Penguin, Harmondsworth, 1977.
Phoenix: The Posthumous Papers, 1936, edited by Edward D. McDonald, Penguin, Harmondsworth, 1978.
Phoenix II: Uncollected, Unpublished, and Other Prose Works, edited by Warren Roberts and Harry T. Moore, Penguin, Harmondsworth, 1978.

Place of publication for the following is London unless otherwise stated:

p. 12 'Where does one . . .' etc: respectively, *Letters* Vol. 6 p. 617; Vol. 7 p. 80; Vol. 7 p. 105.

p. 18 'I don't care . . .': *Letters* Vol. 6 p. 609.

p. 18 'I *don't* like . . .': *ibid* p. 617.

p. 20 'Already I am . . .': *Selected Letters*, Quartet, 1988 p. 98.

p. 21 'I have often . . .': *ibid* p. 74.

p. 23 'Life is more . . .': this starts out as a quotation from 'Reflections on the Death of a Porcupine', *Phoenix II* p. 468.

p. 28 'the Italians are . . .': *Letters* Vol. 3 p. 534.

p. 33 'the intoxication of . . .': *The Gay Science*, Vintage, New York, 1974 p. 32.

p. 33 'existence was one . . .': Introduction to *The Letters of D. H. Lawrence*, Heinemann, 1932 p. xxx.

p. 33 'the long convalescence . . .': *Selected Letters* p. 187.

p. 34 'Michelet wrote nothing . . .': *Michelet*, Hill & Wang, New York, 1987 p. 87.

p. 34 Brodsky: 'To Please a Shadow', in *Less Than One*, Penguin, Harmondsworth, 1987 p. 373.

pp. 35–6 'I hate photographs . . .': *Letters* Vol. 7 p. 189.

p. 37 'I've been seedy . . .': *Letters* Vol. 2 p. 224.

p. 37 'I send a . . .': *Letters* Vol. 5 p. 327.
p. 37 'clean-shaven, bright young . . .': *Letters* Vol. 7 p. 620.
p. 37 Yourcenar: *Memoirs of Hadrian*, Penguin, Harmondsworth, 1959 p. 16.
p. 38 'I had to . . .': *Letters* Vol. 7 p. 646.
p. 38 'Jo Davidson came . . .': *Letters* Vol. 7 p. 653.
p. 38 'What do I . . .': *Phoenix* p. 232.
p. 78 'an accident in . . .': 'Nottingham and the Mining Countryside', *Phoenix* p. 133.
p. 78 'the condemning of . . .': *ibid* p. 138.
p. 78 'but a blind . . .': *ibid*.
pp. 79–80 'If you're in . . .': *Letters* Vol. 5 p. 592.
p. 81 'Pull down my . . .': *Phoenix* p. 140.
p. 82 'he also needs . . .': *Selected Essays and Notebooks*, Penguin, Harmondsworth, 1979 p. 282.
p. 82 'the human soul . . .': *Phoenix* p. 138.
p. 84 'Whatever I forget . . .': *Letters* Vol. 6 p. 618.
p. 84 'I am not . . .': *ibid* p. 535.
p. 84 'walking through the . . .': *op cit* p. 148.
p. 86 'the great free . . .': *ibid* p. 70.
p. 88 'I feel I . . .': *Letters* Vol. 6 p. 182.
p. 88 'will to write . . .': *Letters* Vol. 5 p. 621.
p. 89 'that one thing . . .': Rainer Maria Rilke, *Selected Letters* p. 143.
p. 89 'Either happiness or . . .': *ibid* p. 10.
p. 90 '*Du mußt dein* . . .': from 'Archaic Torso of Apollo', *The Selected Poetry of Rainer Maria Rilke*, edited and translated by Stephen Mitchell, Vintage International, New York, 1989 p. 6.
p. 90 'i.e. find a different . . .': *Selected Letters*, edited by Anthony Thwaite, Faber, 1992 p. 315.

p. 90 'ancient enmity between . . .': *Selected Poetry*, p. 87.
p. 90 'For one human . . .': *ibid* p. 306.
p. 90 'Fidelity to oneself . . .': *Letters* Vol. 4 p. 308.
p. 90 'I don't sacrifice . . .': *Letters* Vol. 5 p. 75.
pp. 90–91 'not the work . . .': *Thomas Hardy* p. 12.
p. 91 'I *don't* think . . .': *Letters* Vol. 3 p. 215.
p. 94 'in the moment . . .': Walter Benjamin, 'A Small History of Photography' in *One Way Street*, Verso, 1979 p. 245.
p. 95 'the tree's life . . .': 'Pan in America', *Phoenix* p. 25.
p. 95 'Thank God I . . .': *Letters* Vol. 4 p. 307.
p. 95 'It is hard . . .': *Selected Letters* p. 157.
p. 95 'no life without . . .': from 'Lullaby of Cape Cod', *A Part of Speech*, Oxford University Press, Oxford, 1980 p.113.
pp. 95–6 'I feel a . . .': *Letters* Vol. 4 p. 301.
p. 96 'One can no . . .': *Letters* Vol. 5 p. 266.
p. 96 'meant nothing to . . .': Rainer Maria Rilke, *Selected Letters* p. 30.
p. 96 'Whisper to the . . .': *Selected Poetry* p. 255.
p. 97 'happy as a . . .': Vincent Van Gogh, *The Letters*, selected and edited by Ronald De Leeuw, Allen Lane, 1996 p. 361.
p. 97 'convinced that every . . .': *Letters* Vol. 5 p. 436.
p. 97 'Perhaps there remains . . .': *The Selected Poetry* p. 151.
p. 98 'A fine wind . . .': *Poems* p. 29.
p. 99 'You mustn't look . . .': *Letters* Vol. 2 p. 183.
p. 102 'The best readings . . .': *Real Presences*, Faber, 1989 p.17.
p. 102 'syllabus of enacted . . .': *ibid* p. 20.
p. 103 'very thorough in . . .': *Letters* Vol. 5 p. 473.
p. 103 'the judgment may . . .': *Sea and Sardinia*, Penguin, Harmondsworth, 1944 p. 131.
p. 107 'Blair has been . . .': *Letters* Vol. 7 p. 641.
p. 109 'she lifted her . . .': *Letters* Vol. 3 p. 40.

p. 110 'Now it is . . .': *Poems* p. 716.
p. 110 'apples on tall . . .': *Letters* Vol. 7 p. 455, discussed by Sagar in *D. H. Lawrence: Life into Art*, Penguin, Harmondsworth, 1985 p. 341.
p. 110 'it is just . . .': *Letters* Vol. 2 p. 692.
p. 110 'the apples blown . . .': *Letters* Vol. 3 p. 216.
p. 110 'seems already a . . .': *Letters* Vol. 5 p. 282.
pp. 111–12 'Since Lawrence died . . .': quoted by Janet Byrne in *A Genius for Living*, Bloomsbury, 1995 p. 376.
p. 112 'Whoever reads me . . .': *Letters* Vol. 5 p. 201.
p. 112 'What do I . . .': *Phoenix* p. 232.
p. 113 'I enjoy looking . . .': quoted by Janet Byrne p. 376.
p. 114 'tapping out an . . .': 'Elegy: D. H. Lawrence' in *The Essential Rebecca West*, Penguin, Harmondsworth, 1983 p. 392.
p. 114 'I feel there . . .': *Letters* Vol. 4 p. 304.
pp. 114–15 'When I drive . . .': *Letters* Vol. 2 p. 431.
p. 114 'wearied himself to . . .': Penguin, Harmondsworth, 1950, p. 33.
p. 115 'always be a . . .': *ibid* p. 434
pp. 115–16 'So vivid a . . .': *ibid* pp. 459–60.
p. 119 'not so much . . .': *Letters* Vol. 4 p. 235.
p. 119 'The land is . . .': *ibid* p. 238.
p. 119 'Have you noticed . . .': Vol. 2, Penguin, Harmondsworth, p. 508.
p. 120 'the one bright . . .': 'Why the Novel Matters', *Phoenix* p. 535.
p. 120 'the highest form . . .': 'The Novel', *Phoenix II* p. 416.
p. 120 'In our time . . .': *op cit* p. 383.
p. 121 'Their freedom of . . .': *Testaments Betrayed*, Faber, 1995 p. 160.

p. 121 'a new art . . .': *The Art of the Novel*, Faber, 1988 p. 65.
p. 121 'A book which . . .': *Letters* Vol. 2 p. 479.
p. 123 'One's native land . . .': *Letters* Vol. 5 p. 312.
p. 125 'the least reticent . . .': *op cit* p. 166.
p. 129 'This is a . . .': *Damn You, England*, Faber, 1994 pp. 193–4.
p. 129 'living in a . . .': *ibid* p. 15.
p. 129 'the root of . . .': *ibid* p. 195.
p. 130 'Curse you, my . . .': *Letters* Vol. 1 p. 424.
p. 130 'I curse my . . .': *Letters* Vol. 3 p. 92.
p. 130 'If thine eye . . .': *Letters* Vol. 2 p. 414.
p. 131 Volentieri: quoted by Paul Carter in *Living in a New Country*, Faber, 1992 p. 154.
p. 132 'It is the . . .': *Letters* Vol. 5 p. 495.
p. 132 'We can so . . .': 'Requiem for a Friend', *The Selected Poetry* p. 85.
p. 132 'The tragedy of . . .': Penguin, Harmondsworth, 1961 p. 212.
p. 133 'from *The Rainbow* . . .': quoted by Janet Byrne p. 411.
pp. 133–4 'sick with fatigue' etc.: Penguin, Harmondsworth, 1960 pp. 149–51.
p. 134 'I looked down . . .': *ibid* p. 158.
p. 134 'the dangerous privilege . . .': Cambridge University Press, Cambridge, 1986 p. 8.
p. 135 'To know serenity . . .': *Engaging Form*, Cape, 1988 p. 85.
p. 136 'He who returns . . .': 'Adioses', *Plenos Poderes*, Losada, Buenos Aires, 1962 p. 461.
p. 136 'I feel I . . .': *Letters* Vol. 4 p. 263.
p. 136 'grew together as . . .': Cape, 1987 p. 50.
p. 136 'Oh Schwiegermutter it . . .': *Letters* Vol. 4 p. 238.

p. 137 'This place no . . .': *Letters* Vol. 7 p. 651.
p. 138 'Either you go . . .': *Letters* Vol. 5 p. 170.
p. 138 'Freedom is a . . .': *ibid* p. 191.
p. 139 'he did nothing . . .': quoted by Rebecca West p. 395.
p. 139 *'you've always done . . .'*: 'The Life with a Hole in It', *Collected Poems*, edited by Anthony Thwaite, Faber, 1988 p. 202.
p. 139 'My wife and . . .': *Letters* Vol. 3 p. 734.
p. 139 'The only history . . .': *Letters* Vol. 2 p. 161.
p. 139 'We had almost . . .': *Letters* Vol. 4 p. 175.
p. 140 'It is my . . .': *Letters* Vol. 4 p. 238.
p. 140 'Really, why does . . .': *Letters* Vol. 7 p. 165.
p. 140 'Each one of . . .': Faber, 1987 p. 48.
p. 141 'Basically it's none . . .': *Letters on Cézanne*, Cape, 1989 p. 8.
p. 141 'Naturally I don't . . .': *Letters* Vol. 5 p. 45.
p. 141 'I have painted . . .': *ibid* p. 570.
pp. 141–2 'Lawrence was always . . .': quoted by Janet Byrne p. 310.
p. 142 'the washing, cooking . . .': *Letters* Vol. 4 p. 111.
p. 144 'By now, it . . .': 'Fine Adjustments', *Acrimony*, Faber, 1986 p. 77.
p. 145 *'The photograph* . . .': *Letters* Vol. 5 p. 208.
p. 147 'I owe you . . .': *Letters* Vol. 2 p. 505.
p. 147 'remind Frieda . . .': 'Of course Frieda . . .': *ibid* p. 654 and p. 658.
p. 147 'can't help feeling . . .': *Letters* Vol. 6 p. 542.
p. 148 'I am thoroughly . . .': *Sea and Sardinia*, p. 28.
p. 148 'Does the return . . .': *Letters* Vol. 4 pp. 375–6.
p. 148 'I don't want . . .': *Letters* Vol. 3 p. 519.
p. 149 'everybody is hard . . .': *The Letters 1857–1880*, edited

by Francis Steegmuller, Harvard, Cambridge, 1982 p. 156.
p. 149 'to absorb himself . . .': *op cit* p. xxxi.
p. 150 'painting and fucking . . .': *op cit* p. 365.
p. 151 'Painting is a . . .': *Letters* Vol. 5 p. 619.
pp. 151–2 'an even more . . .': *op cit* p. xxvi.
p. 153 'I shall turn . . .': I have departed slightly from Walter Kaufmann's translation of this line from *The Gay Science* p. 223.
pp. 156–7 'No, I don't . . .'etc.: *Letters* Vol. 4 p. 108.
pp. 157–8 'I feel my . . .': *ibid* p. 98.
p. 158 'marvellous air, marvellous . . .': *ibid* p. 239.
p. 158 'If all goes . . .': *Selected Letters* p. 192.
pp. 158–9 'the life-exhaustion feeling . . .': *Letters* Vol. 4 p. 189.
p. 159 'no life of . . .': *ibid* p. 406.
p. 159 'Suddenly that I . . .': *ibid* p. 168.
p. 159 'people who rave . . .': *Letters* Vol. 7 p. 489.
p. 159 'one of those . . .': *Letters* Vol. 4 p. 113.
pp. 159–60 'one does *nothing* . . .': *Sea and Sardinia* p. 76.
p. 160 'of more and . . .': quoted by Sagar p. 354.
p. 160 'So Mabel thought . . .': Brenda Maddox, *The Married Man*, Sinclair-Stevenson, 1994 p. 367.
p. 160 Magris: *Danube*, Collins Harvill, 1989 p. 77.
p. 161 'a black ribbon . . .': *Letters* Vol. 2 p. 621.
p. 161 'is just twice . . .': *ibid* p. 622.
p. 161 'exactly like the . . .': *ibid* p. 636.
p. 162 'it got on . . .': *ibid* p. 637.
p. 162 'Never will I . . .': *ibid* p. 638.
p. 162 'Many thanks for . . .': *ibid* p. 638.
p. 162 'But always remember . . .': *Letters* Vol. 3 p. 595.
pp. 162–3 'More and more . . .': *Letters* Vol. 4 p. 154.

p. 163 'for the first . . .': *ibid* p. 170.
p. 163 'I only know . . .': *ibid* p. 170.
p. 163 'and his rat-hole . . .': *ibid* p. 234.
p. 163 'I am essentially . . .': *Letters* Vol. 5 p. 67.
p. 164 'My business is . . .': *Letters* Vol. 6 p. 72.
p. 164 'All truth – and . . .': *Letters* Vol. 5 p. 519.
p. 164 'But I do . . .': *Letters* Vol. 7 p. 574.
p. 164 'One no longer . . .': *op cit* p. 355.
p. 165 'For my part . . .': *Letters* Vol. 7 p. 616.
p. 165 'very nice to . . .': *Letters* Vol. 6 p. 148.
p. 165 'that stillness in . . .': *Letters* Vol. 7 p. 235.
p. 165 'sitting in the . . .': *ibid* p. 211.
p. 166 'It is very . . .': *ibid* p. 510.
p. 166 Carey: *The Intellectuals and the Masses*, Faber, 1992, particularly pp. 10–12 and 75–80.
p. 166 'struggle inside . . .': *Letters* Vol. 2 p. 161.
p. 167 'never finish making . . .': *The Rebel*, Penguin, Harmondsworth, 1962, p. 67.
p. 167 'both their wretchedness . . .': 'Summer in Algiers', *Selected Essays and Notebooks* p. 81.
p. 167 'only one thing . . .': 'Summer in Algiers', *op cit* pp. 89–90.
p. 167 'slightly intoxicated': *Selected Letters* p. 67.
p. 168 'If the Greeks . . .': 'Helen's Exile', *Selected Essays and Notebooks* p. 136.
p. 168 'there is no . . .': 'Love of Life', *ibid* p. 60.
p. 168 'in the most . . .': *The Gay Science* p. 242.
p. 168 'the double damnation . . .': *Selected Essays and Notebooks* p. 19.
p. 168 'Never to wish . . .': I have set down Nietzsche's ideal of *amor fati* like this because this is exactly how I remember it,

even though I have remembered it – from R. J. Hollingdale's translation – slightly inaccurately: *cf. Ecce Homo*, Penguin, Harmondsworth, 1979 p. 68.

p. 170 'beastly Oaxaca': *Letters* Vol. 5 p. 235.

p. 172 'Poor Bertie Russell . . .': quoted by Harry T. Moore in *The Priest of Love*, Penguin, Harmondsworth, 1976 p. 516.

p. 174 'To be brave . . .': Epilogue to *Movements in European History*, Oxford University Press, Oxford, 1981 p. 308.

p. 174 'men who give . . .': *Into Their Labours*, Granta, 1992 p. 329.

p. 180 'malaria – with grippe . . .': *Letters* Vol. 5 p. 230.

p. 187 'very pleasant' and 'very beautiful': *Letters* Vol. 5, respectively p. 163 and p. 177.

p. 189 'Let a man . . .': *Letters* Vol. 3 p. 21.

p. 189 'a mere wreck . . .': *Letters* Vol. 5 p. 230.

p. 189 'so foul one . . .': *Letters* Vol. 3 p. 55.

p. 199 'Don't for heaven's . . .': *Letters* Vol. 6 p. 535.

p. 208 'it would be . . .': *Letters* Vol. 5 p. 585.

p. 215 'old nodality': 'Taos', *Phoenix*, p. 100.

p. 219 'I am no . . .': *Sea and Sardinia* p. 49.

p. 222 'Cars of women . . .': quoted by Janet Byrne p. 385.

p. 225 'Think of the . . .': *The Complete Poems 1927–1979*, Noonday Press/ Farrar, Straus and Giroux, New York, 1983 pp. 93–4.

p. 225 'What is it . . .': *Letters* Vol. 5 p. 196.

p. 225 'Why can't one . . .' and 'Why does one . . .': *Sea and Sardinia*, respectively, p. 1 and p. 3.

p. 227 'a prisoner deprived . . .': *The Book of Disquiet*, Quartet, 1991 p. 125.

p. 229 'able to stifle . . .': *op cit* p. 80.